THE MYSTERY OF
THE DUKE OF PERTH

A historical enigma

Arthur App

Foreword

The Duke of Perth fled from the disastrous defeat at the Battle of Culloden in 1746. He took a ship to France but died from his wounds before he arrived. He died childless. That's a fact. It's in the history books.

So, how come that same Duke of Perth's grandson is buried in a graveyard in a small village by the River Wear in the north-east of England? That's a fact. It says on the headstone that he died in 1873.

It's a mystery. A mystery that engaged the mind of journalist Arthur Appleton. For thirty years he patiently gathered evidence and tried to unravel the curious case. Finally he presented his findings in his lucid and entertaining journalist style. The resulting book was almost ready for publication when Arthur was taken ill and died. The sadness is that he didn't live to see this delightful book in print.

For Arthur this investigation was a marathon effort. It's been my privilege to pick up the baton and carry it those last few yards over the finishing line.

Arthur's talents for research and for writing are wonderfully preserved here. This book is his monument. I'd like to think he'd be pleased with that thought.

Terry Deary

Contents

Chapter 1
Truth or False Belief

The graveyard

Once I planned to write a romantic novel which would accept that James Drummond, the 3rd Duke (and 6th Earl) of Perth, after the shock of the defeat at Culloden and the collapse of the Jacobite cause, recovered from his wounds in a pitman's cottage at Biddick on the Wear, married the beautiful daughter of the pitman, and evaded the executioner's axe by living the rest of his life in obscurity.

James Drummond hid for much of the second half of the eighteenth century in the village of Biddick until his death in 1782. However, no one was seeking him, as it was presumed on some evidence, that he had died on shipboard when escaping to France in May 1746, a month after Culloden.

All Saints Church, Penshaw, built as a chapel of ease to the parish church of St Michael's at Houghton-le-Spring, is 'a plain building with nothing ecclesiastical in its character,' says Fordyce the historian. It was endowed in 1754 and stands withdrawn up the valley side from South Biddick, in the lee of Penshaw Hill, although for many years its site must have been prominent.

I remembered seeing the Duke of Perth's gravestone there years ago. Not the 3rd Duke who was in command of the Jacobite left wing on awesome Drummossie Moor at Culloden, and of the sieges of Carlisle and Stirling, the lieutenant general in the brief horrible sword slashing at Prestonpans, and the leader of the night attack across Dornoch Firth; not the 3rd Duke of Perth, Lord Elcho's 'very brave and gallant man,' or 'the noblest Jacobite of all,' (as a present-day Perthshire historian proclaims) although his bones lie near. It was the grave of his grandson, Thomas Drummond, a pitman of New Penshaw who nearly succeeded in gaining the title and the estates.

And reading his case, one can think that he should have succeeded.

I have been back there to see the stone. Old Penshaw village is now the posh end of Penshaw. The thick undergrowth in the churchyard has gone, and hurrying over the spaces between the isolated gravestones I feared that the Duke's stone had fallen. However a railed right-of-way bisects the churchyard and at the other side I found the grave. It can be seen from the right-of-way path.

I was wrong about having seen the "Duke of Perth" on the stone. I have written an autobiography in which memory could be checked by journal entries, and I know that memory can twist away from reality, leaving the subconscious to implant what one likes to believe. The stone, in fact, is not solely personal: proclaiming family pride it is headed 'The Burial Place of the Drummond Family.' The Dukedom is not mentioned, but the Earldom is.

The long inscription on the inclined greened stone, black smudged in places, gives the names of eight children, six female and two male, who died while their parents lived, the eldest young woman thirty-three and the elder young man thirty-two. Their mother Jane died in 1871 aged seventy-seven, and, with the wording becoming squeezed, there it was,
'Thomas Drummond the rightful heir to the Earldom of Perth who died November (the date is indecipherable) 1873 aged 81 years.'

Next to it there is a smaller more upright and greener stone which continues the recording of the dying of the young. Six grandchildren of Thomas and Jane, the eldest twenty-two, dying between 1858 and 1872, the children of a surviving son, also called Thomas and his wife Margaret.

The Fordyce story

The tale of the Biddick Duke of Perth did not become generally known until 1826 when the claim for the title and the estates was being prepared. That is forty-four years after the Biddick Duke's death. His first-born son, James, who died in 1823, declined to claim, even though in 1784, two years after the death of his father, the annexation of the forfeited estates was lifted to enable them to be granted to the heir.

In 1827-28 the tale was stated as fact in The History, Directory and Gazetteer of the Counties of Northumberland and Durham by Parson and White.

"It was here (Biddick) the unfortunate James Drummond, commonly called Duke of Perth, took sanctuary after the rebellion of 1745-46, under the protection of Nicholas Lambton, Esq. of South Biddick, where he lived in obscurity and concealment till 1782 when he died and was buried at Painshaw."

It was also given as fact in one of the admirable nineteenth-century histories of County Durham, that of William Fordyce, published in 1855. Fordyce gives the core story:

"The sequestered village of South Biddick was the asylum of the attainted Duke of Perth; and here, in the humblest circumstances, since the disastrous and memorable rebellion of 1745, the descendants of that unfortunate nobleman have remained."

The Duke, Fordyce said, had caused a report to be circulated that he had died from wounds and fatigue when escaping on a ship bound for France, but in fact he had boarded a different ship which brought him to South Shields from where he made his way to Sunderland and then up river to Biddick where John Armstrong, a pitman, gave him shelter and care. Later he was to give him a lovely bride. For Armstrong's twelve-year old daughter, Elizabeth, was "a girl of exquisite beauty and of artless and most engaging manners," and when she was sixteen or seventeen, the Duke, then thirty-six, married her at Houghton-le-Spring parish church, St Michael's.

Afterwards Nicholas Lambton of Biddick Hall granted them the occupation of a cottage, the Boat House, saying, "I know you well enough; you are one of the Drummonds, the rebels; but I will give you the house and garden for all that."

A daughter of the couple, Elizabeth (later Mrs Peters) remembered this being said. The Biddick Duke became the local ferryman, and his wife ran a small shop. They were poor and their second child, and first boy, also called James, joined his grandfather down the pit, to his father's dismay. The 1771 floods wrecked their home and among the possessions swept away was a wooden box or chest containing irreplaceable family papers. Mrs Peters said her father kept searching the banks of the river.

After nearly thirty years, the Biddick Duke, in disguise, revisited his old home, Drummond Castle, near Crieff, still held by the Crown. He was recognised by some of the tenants and given hospitality. He died at the age of sixty-nine. (His burial entry in the All Saints' register maintains the secrecy and could not be simpler: 'James Drummond of Biddick 10th June 1782.' No age is given.)

Fordyce continues that when, in 1784, the annexation of the Drummond estates ended, and there was no claim from the elder son, James, his younger brother, William, determined to do something about it. William had gone to sea and was doing rather well. He took what papers there still were on his father's title but his ship was run down and he was drowned. The vital papers were lost.

James died in 1823. His eldest son, Thomas, born on 3rd April 1792, also a pitman, eventually claimed the Earldom and on the "20th June 1831 at the Canongate Court Room, Edinburgh, Thomas Drummond of Biddick in the county of Durham, grandson and last heir male of the body of James, 6th Earl of Perth, commonly called the 'Duke of Perth,' was, by a respectable jury, unanimously served nearest and lawful heir."

However in 1785 the estates had been granted to another branch of the family, and Thomas's claim at the Court of Session in Edinburgh for the title and lands was turned down: the status quo being upheld on the supposition that James Drummond the Duke of Perth had died without issue in 1746.

That is the story outline, followed by Fordyce,

The Mackenzie and Ross story

The writer in one of the other voluminous Durham county histories, that of Mackenzie and Ross, published in 1834 (earlier than that of Fordyce) is objective and not so emotionally involved despite writing before the Court of Session verdict in 1835, and also recording evidence which seemed to prove beyond doubt that Thomas's claim should have succeeded.

South Biddick, he says, had some ten shops or houses where contraband spirits were sold without licence, and then adds, not factually as Fordyce was to do, that, 'Here, it is said, James Drummond, generally styled Duke of Perth, sought shelter and safety after the defeat of Prince Charles at Culloden.'

The tentativeness about the title stems from the fact that the Dukedom was granted by James II to the 3rd Duke's grandfather, (the 4th Earl) in 1693, after King James had been deposed as king and was holding court at St Germain in France. The 1st Duke, the most illustrious of the Drummonds, had been Lord High Chancellor of Scotland, appointed by Charles II. The Dukedom granted by a deposed king had no validity in Britain, unless the

Stuarts were restored as monarchs.

The 3rd Duke, born 11th May 1713, came into the title when a child after his father, who had taken part in the 1715 Jacobite rising, escaped to France only to die there. The 3rd Duke's mother, daughter of the Duke of Gordon, was a fervent Stuart supporter, and had him educated and brought up in France. About the time of his majority he returned to Scotland, and in 1745, joined the rebellion of Prince Charles Edward (popularly known as Bonnie Prince Charlie) and the chieftains. After Culloden, which was on 16th April the following year, "according to common opinion," he embarked for France and died on the passage.

But, says the Mackenzie/Ross history, in Thomas Drummond's claim this common opinion is denied, and it is said that after Culloden the 3rd Duke hid in the woods of his castle and then sailed for Shields.

His two daughters, Mrs Ann Atkinson and Mrs Elizabeth Peters, declared that they had heard both General Lambton and Nicholas Lambton refer to their father as "the rebel Drummond." Then comes the seemingly irrefutable proof: a letter to the Duke in county Durham from his younger brother, Lord John Drummond, from Boulogne, written on 16th April 1747, the first anniversary of the battle of Culloden. Lord John had escaped to France and, on the generally accepted death of his brother, had become the 4th Duke and 7th Earl, He wrote, 'I think you had better come to France, and you would be out of danger, as I find you are living in obscurity at Houghton-le-Spring.'

The story broke too late for inclusion in William Hutchinson's remarkable three-volume pioneer history published between 1785 and 1794, and also missed the renowned Surtees' history. Surtees died in 1834 when busy with his fourth volume.

He provided Sir Walter Scott with material. Scott in *Tales of a Grandfather* tells of the Duke of Perth evading capture at Drummond Castle, and, I think, if he had known of the later story could well have written at length about the Duke at Biddick. Scott visited Surtees at Mainsforth Hall. On the occasion of a reception for Scott in Sunderland, Surtees saw Scott in front of him and laying a hand on his shoulder whispered two lines of an old ballad. Without glancing round Scott said, 'That must be my Surtees.'

Biddick Village

The people of South Biddick carried a stigma of lawlessness for years. As late as 1893 the first headmaster of the new school at North Biddick across the river pleaded successfully that Biddick should not be part of the name.

Frederick Hill, a Washington teacher, pulled together what had been written, stopping short at original research. He said so many malefactors made for Biddick that it was known as Britain's Botany Bay and that Botany Bay was even registered as a place of birth and death. The name, corrupted, of the Australian penal colony survived into the twentieth century when North Biddick Colliery was known as Buttany Pit. Until late in the nineteenth century "Go to Biddick," approached equality with "Go to Hell."

Much of Hill's information came from an article by J R Boyle in the 1889 edition of the Monthly Chronicle of North-country Lore and Legend. Boyle gave more of the crucial 1747 letter to the Duke from his brother, Lord John Drummond: "I think you had better come to France, as you would be out of danger, as I find you are living in obscurity at Houghton-le-Spring. I doubt that is a dangerous place yet. You say it is reported you died on your passage to France. I hope and trust you will still live in obscurity." Boyle said the brothers continued to correspond.

Boyle also gave details of the Duke's property lost in the 1771 flood. In the wooden box swept away there was a tanned leather pouch with three pockets and in these were the Duke's memorandum book, family papers, including letters, a deed Patent of Nobility and a diamond ring. Boyle/Hill say that the Duke visited Scotland more than once in disguise, although the only visit furnished with detail is the last one.

Hill says it was believed locally that the Duke's pitman son, James, was employed at (but not down) the Row Pit at the time of the explosion there on 30th June 1817. Forty-six men and boys were killed, eight men during rescue work. One family called Hill lost ten males: grandfather, two sons and seven grandsons, aged 15, 14, 12, 11, 10, 9 and 8. James Drummond would be about sixty-five then, so he could well have had a surface job. Boyle/Hill also tell of Thomas Drummond's drunkenness prior to his appearance before the House of Lords, behaviour which lost him the support of Lord Durham.

Their accounts fade away unsurely, unsatisfactorily. The telling of the lore and legend was their objective, not an investigation.

The Third Duke

The Third Duke of Perth was six foot tall, slender and not physically strong. His health was never consistently good, which suggests that the bravery he maintained during the Forty-five was even more admirable. His French was better than his English, and he often indulged in broad Scots. He could become animated and 'a little prolix.' He was generally liked and respected, even loved. An inscription in the kirkyard at Cumbernauld reads:

Oh hold me not, my mother earth,
But raise me with the Duke of Perth,
With many another local lad,
Once more to wear the white cockade.

Thomas Drummond's claim that he was indeed the grandson of this man, that he was the 8th Earl of Perth, was persuasive. Apart from the Hanoverian Major-General Lambton, the Lambtons were sympathetic, including, it seems, John George who became the 1st Earl of Durham and Governor-General of Canada. The lawyers who probed and worked without fee or expenses in the early days, although perhaps with some remuneration later when subscriptions came in, obviously thought they had an excellent chance of winning and that after their legal victory they would be liberally rewarded.

So, a powerful case. But the one it had to defeat was also powerful. And behind it there could be another mystery. If the man at Biddick wasn't the Duke, why should he say he was and court seizure and execution? If he was the Duke he was an attainted man, already judged attainted of high treason, without trial, in the Attainder Act of 1746.

If he was not the Duke, who was he?

Chapter 2
Chivvying the common pitman

William Fitz Strathern's investigations

The marshalling of the Biddick Claimant's case began in 1826. There had been a foray prior to this. That was in 1806, just more than twenty years after the handing-back of the estates to the Drummond family, in the person of a Captain James Drummond, later Lord Perth. The two daughters of the Biddick Duke, Anne Atkinson and Elizabeth Peters, saw and talked to Captain James's widow and daughter.

When they made a second approach the widow and daughter refused to see them. Elizabeth Peters would want her revenge for that snub.

In July 1826 an appeal for help was made by Henry Ingledew, solicitor, of Dean Street, Newcastle, on behalf of Thomas Drummond "at present in the lowest situation of life although entitled by his birth and lineage to the rank of nobility. He earns a hard livelihood by working as a common pitman in New Painshaw Colliery." Ingledew supported his appeal with an open letter from William Fitz Strathern, Law Genealogist, of 6 Barnard's Inn, London.

Fitz Strathern said that encouraged by the Biddick Claimant's aunt, Mrs Peters, and by the prospect of reward later, he had been investigating in Scotland for months at his own expense. Mrs Peters' exertions for her nephew Thomas could not be too much praised, and he hoped that Ingledew would convince the young man to make, for the first time, some substantial exertion for his own cause. (The young man, born 3rd April 1792 would be thirty-four, and had been married for eleven years, since 14th May 1815, to Jane Burn of Newbottle, and was the father of four or five children.) So it was not a case of Thomas, the grandson, initiating determined action when the way was clear after the death of his father: it was his aunt Elizabeth, the Biddick Duke's second daughter, who was bestirring matters.

Fitz Strathern asserted that were a sufficiency of funds impressed in his hands he would most likely get Thomas passed as Earl of Perth in the ensuing parliament. He had seen Thomas' sister, Hannah, 'a very sensible young woman,' and had told her the cause of the delay.

Why had he not seen Thomas? Was Thomas a reluctant nobleman, made uneasy by his aunt's insistence. Was he keeping out of the way, scared to be taken into a world of lawyers and upper class people to face social confrontations in which he would feel inferior, be inferior, at times deliberately made to feel so. He would be unable to express himself, indeed have little to express, in a world in which he would speak inadequately and roughly, using the only words he knew, words which the superior people would scarcely understand?

Fitz Strathern wanted to purchase a brief from his Majesty's Chancery in Scotland, and then, by a respectable jury of Scotch gentlemen, to serve Thomas heir of male and line to his great-great-grandfather, the 1st Duke, and his great-grandfather, the 2nd Duke.

Thomas's claim rested on the identity of his grandfather, and it would be necessary to take Mrs Peters to Scotland to prove that. "The poor woman, although advanced in years, [she would be sixty-two], is willing to go north to serve not only her brother's family or rather to serve the clan Drummond, which is in want of a chief, and were she possessed of the means her nephew would already have been served heir this summer, not however without previously acquainting him of it." (How Thomas must have kept out of the way.)

When two registers were obtained from France and three from Durham, Thomas's pedigree would be complete. An act of parliament would be passed in his favour leading to the restoration of family titles, honours and dignities and, Fitz Strathern trusted, the estates, which, had his father come forward in 1785 when the government advertised for the heirs, would have been given back to the family then. However it was clear that Thomas would never be preferred to the titles if Mrs Peters died without proving her father's identity. It would take about one hundred pounds of expenses to obtain the identity and French registers. "All the rest was plain sailing." The Chancellor of Durham, the Reverend Mr Baker, had given him five pounds towards the expenses, which was all the money he had ever received.

The letter in the press

A letter followed in the press as from Thomas Drummond, dated 22nd September 1826.

It said that James Drummond, the 1st Duke, who died at St Germain in 1716, made a resignation, as early as 1687, of the Earldom and his whole estate to his eldest son, James, Lord Drummond who became the 2nd Duke. This son was engaged in the 1715 rebellion and escaped to France in 1716 in the same vessel as the Pretender, James, the son of the deposed James II. The 2nd Duke was attainted, but again the estate was saved for the family, as in 1713 he had executed a deed of entail to his eldest son, which was later sustained by the Court of Session in Edinburgh and affirmed by the House of Lords. He died in 1720 and was succeeded by his eldest son, again called James, the one commonly known as the 3rd Duke of Perth, who took part in the 1745 rebellion.

The letter says the 3rd Duke escaped to France after Culloden where he remained for two or three years before coming to England and settling in the County of Durham. With a view to saving him from capture it was given out that he had died: in one account he was said to have died at Culloden, in another on the passage to France.

The Biddick Duke married in 1749. His eldest son, James Drummond (father of the present claimant) born in 1752, and consigned to work in a coal mine, was now dead.

The letter pointed out that genealogy was perfect, the existence and depository of all documents known and of easy attainment. A few hundred pounds were needed. Should such generosity place the claimant in the situation he looked for, his first act should be to refund, but should the result be unsuccessful, then his thanks must be all that he could bestow. Subscriptions were to be sent to Fitz Strathern or Ingledew, or to named banking houses in Newcastle, London and Edinburgh.

This was the 1826 letter in the press. There are two things of note in it.

Firstly, one could wonder why the 3rd Duke of Perth should come to England when he was safe in France. Why leave friends, places, a way of life he knew, closeness to Jacobite affairs, for the alien land and life of Biddick? And if he had two or three years in France after Culloden, (April 16th 1746), he was limiting the time in which he decided to change his way of living by marrying Elizabeth Armstrong in November 1749.

Secondly, of course, there is no mention at this time of the 1747 letter from his younger brother in France. If the 3rd Duke himself was in France then no such letter would exist.

The idea that the Biddick Duke had gone from Culloden to France and thence to Wearside was quietly dropped from subsequent claims.

The "ignoble assault"

At the end of October a long letter of three thousand words or so appeared in the Tyne Mercury. Signed 'Advocatus Legis', seemingly an English lawyer in Edinburgh, it defended an "ignoble assault" on the Biddick Claimant, Thomas Drummond, in the Berwick Advertiser. Advocatus's defending letter said that had Thomas Drummond's father made a claim in 1785 he would unquestionably have obtained the estates. In the absence of the claim the estates had gone to Captain James Drummond, who had been created Baron Perth and Lord Drummond; on his death the succession had gone to his daughter Lady Gwydyr and her husband.

With wondrous naivety 'Advocatus Legis' then said that such was the immense wealth and plurality of titles possessed by Lord and Lady Gwydyr, that as soon as proofs of legitimacy were established, they would see the moral justice, the decency and propriety of relinquishing these additional honours and estates to a poor kinsman, the rightful heir and chief of the Clan Drummond.

But a worrying point against the Biddick Claimant, Thomas, was mentioned - the standing and power conferred by long-term possession. The "ignoble assault" letter had said there should be no violation of existing rights. 'Advocatus Legis' pointed out that a period of fifty years had not passed, and even supposing the Gwydyrs were so ungenerous as to attempt to avail themselves of the laws of prescription, it should be remembered that the claims of Thomas Drummond had come within that period.

Although not fully explicit, Advocatus revealed the approach of twenty years earlier, in 1806, to Lady Gwydyr by "her poor, destitute female relatives, who applied to her, under peculiar circumstances. Lady Gwydyr, then the Hon. Miss Drummond, after having satisfied herself that they were the issue of the unfortunate Earl of Perth (which, it can be proved, both she and her mother did at the time,) shut the door of compassion on her disconsolate relatives, nor has she, to this day, thought proper to make the least enquiry after them, or to bestow the smallest kindness on any of them."

The female relatives would surely be the two daughters of the Duke: Anne Atkinson and Elizabeth Peters. Anne would be in her mid-fifties in 1806 and Elizabeth in her early forties, so a grown-up daughter or two could well have been with them. This was when their brother James, the male heir, two years younger than Anne, was alive, and is further proof that the impetus to take some action sprang from the daughters. There could well have been family arguments over the matter, perhaps a family split.

Captain James Drummond and the Earldom

There is a report in the periodical *The Berwick Museum*, published in Berwick in 1785, that the grant of the estates of Perth from George III to Captain James Drummond arrived in Edinburgh by express from London on 9th May that year. It did not include the Earldom and other titles.

The Captain was the great grandson of John, Earl of Melfort, brother of James Drummond, the 1st Duke of Perth, the one who was Lord High Chancellor of Scotland and created a Duke by the deposed James II. The estates, forfeited by the attainder of Lord John Drummond, brother to our Duke of Perth, and so vested in the Crown, had been managed by a board of trustees.

The proceeds of the trust were directed to "civilising the inhabitants" of the Highlands, and promoting among them "the Protestant religion, good government, industry and manufactures, and the principles of duty and loyalty to His Majesty." The attainder act of George II stated that before the forfeiture they had stood devised to heirs male, but Lord John Drummond had "died without leaving issue lawful of his body and it is not yet ascertained who is his nearest collateral heir male," but to such the estates would be granted subject to a charge of fifty-two thousand five hundred and forty-seven pounds, one shilling and sixpence, and three twelfths part of a penny sterling to be paid into the Court of the Exchequer. Such sums would be directed in part towards the cost of building the Register House in Edinburgh and to the completion of the Forth and Clyde canal.

There is no reference in this 1785 report to this mighty charge of fifty-two thousand pounds being paid. The knowledgeable 'Advocatus Legis' in his Tyne Mercury letter in October 1826 says not a half-penny did either Captain James Drummond or his son-in-law, Lord Gwydyr, ever pay for the extensive domains. He commented that if either had done so then Biddick Claimant Thomas Drummond must yield up the territorial point.

J R Boyle in the Monthly Chronicle for April 1889 says that the captain paid the charge, and this is repeated by Frederick Hill, the local historian. Neither essayed original research, but even so, unless Boyle assumed it was paid - otherwise the captain could not have taken over the estates - he must have read somewhere that it was. It was never publicly faced by Thomas Drummond's advisers which rather implies that the captain had not paid, if he had, surely, if they were successful in claiming possession of the estates from his daughter, they would have had to reimburse the family. Such a prospect could have overpowered them at the start.

The captain had no male children. His daughter, Clementina Sarah, after her marriage was known as Lady Gwydyr, and later Lady Willoughby de Eresby. In 1792 a letter in the Gentlemen's Magazine signed 'Inquisitor' could well have been written by him or on his behalf. It enquired for "any information concerning a charter granted by James II in 1687 to the Earl of Perth extending the title to Heirs general. As it is of consequence a good reward would be given for the discovery of this deed, or a copy of it." It seems that no such deed extending the title to daughters was forthcoming.

In September that year the Newcastle Chronicle reported that James Drummond of Perth had claimed the ancient honours of Earl of Perth, Lord Stobhall and Baron Montefex. He became known as Baron Perth and Lord Drummond. In Henrietta Tayler's Jacobite Epilogue he is listed as titular 11th Earl of Perth. His seemingly formidable daughter could not succeed to a comparative title but she did to possession of the estates, considered by some to be a highly preferable holding.

Preparing the 1828 claim

In November 1826 there was another appeal for subscriptions to enable

Thomas "to assert and prosecute his just and undoubted claim, founded on the most conclusive and incontrovertible evidence." Additional receivers were named in Durham, Leeds and Wakefield.

In December there was an appeal for any remembrance or record of the Biddick Duke attending a Roman Catholic church in County Durham. It was thought that he remained a Catholic and there was evidence that he attended a place of worship, or church, or meeting of the Roman Catholic persuasion, at Chester-le-Street or nearby. No one else in the family was Catholic.
The family churches were St Michael's, Houghton-le-Spring, and from 1754, All Saints at Penshaw. It was said in the appeal that the Duke had been in the area since 1747, so his presumed time in France had been trimmed.

After that, among the lawyers and advisers, there must have been a feeling growing into near-certainty that Thomas's claim would succeed. By late 1828 an impressive document had been assembled: "A statement of the claims of Thomas Drummond to the Ancient Honours and Entailed Estates of the Earldom of Perth, the whole being founded on authentic documents."

In full variety of the printers' craft the statement was published in 1830 by R T Edgar of Pilgrim Street and printed by Mackenzie and Dent of Newcastle making a sixty-page octavo booklet, fronted by an engraving of a drawing of Thomas as a gentleman of the day with fine nose and hair, cravat and coat.

Chapter 3
The Formidable Claim

The 1828 Claim - the background

The written Claim traces the beginning of the Drummond family to a gift of lands, including Drymen or Drummond in Stirlingshire, by Malcolm Canmore, King of Scotland, to a Hungarian, Maurice, who, about the year 1067, helped Edgar Atheling, "the rightful heir to the crown of England," and his sister Margaret to escape from William, Duke of Normandy. The king married Margaret, and Maurice Drummond received a maid of honour in marriage.

In the fourteenth century Annabella Drummond, as wife of Robert III, was Queen of Scotland. Towards the end of the fifteenth century Sir John Drummond became Lord Drummond and had Drummond Castle built. In 1605 the 4th Lord Drummond was created Earl of Perth. The family began suffering because of their allegiance to the Stuarts when under the republican government the 2nd Earl was heavily fined. With the two sons, James and John, of the 3rd Earl, the Drummonds divided into two branches, two Earldoms - the branch of the younger son being that of Melfort.

The 1st Duke of Perth born in 1648 succeeded his father in 1675. Wealthy, well-educated, talented, at thirty he was one of Charles II's privy councillors; and when thirty-six was made Lord High Chancellor of Scotland. (Henry Drummond's Noble British Families says "This period was the apogee of the Drummonds: the head of their house was Lord High Chancellor and Justice General; his brother, the Earl of Melfort, was Secretary of State and Governor of Edinburgh Castle; his brother in law, the Duke of Queensbury, was Lord High Treasurer, and his cousin, Lord Strathallan, was Commander in Chief of the Army.")

On the accession of James II in 1685 the 4th Earl (who was to become the 1st Duke) declared himself a Roman Catholic; as a consequence when the king was deposed in 1688, his house in Edinburgh was plundered and he retreated to Drummond Castle. Eventually he sailed from Kirkcaldy for France, but the vessel was pursued and he and his family taken back to the mainland and imprisoned in Stirling Castle for nearly four years, from 1689 to 1693. When they were released he gave his bond to leave the kingdom. At the exiled court at St Germain-en-Laye he was created Duke of Perth, appointed Knight of the Garter and governor to the Prince of Wales. He married three times and had ten children, six of them male, but by his first wife only one male: James Lord Drummond, father of our Duke at Biddick

James Lord Drummond was educated in France and when eighteen or so accompanied James II on his expedition to Ireland in 1689. He was allowed to stay at Drummond Castle when his father and step-mother were held at Stirling. In the 1715 rising when James III landed in Scotland he supported him, and eventually, like his father - and his son - had to flee the country, joining his father in France. He was attainted of high treason in 1715, but, as his father had done, he had secured the succession for the family by executing an early disposition in favour of his eldest son.

The eldest son, James, the 3rd Duke and 6th Earl, after his French upbringing, came to Drummond Castle in 1732. His brother John, remained behind and entered into the service of the King of France for whom he raised a regiment. During the Forty-five their mother, Lady Jean, was imprisoned in Edinburgh Castle in February 1746. When she was released late that year, the Drummond estates had been taken over by the crown. The Claim blames her for forcing her son to take an active part in the rebellion and says that she never forgave him for his luke-warmness. The latter doesn't make sense, and the former sounds like spurious pleading to partially exonerate the Duke.

The 3rd Duke was born 11th May 1713. The disposition in his favour was dated 28th August 1713, and even though his father was attainted in 1715 the disposition was sustained by the Court of Session in 1719 and affirmed by the House of Lords in 1720.

The 1828 Claim - the Third Duke's escape to Biddick

The Claim said that in 1740 the Duke and his half-uncle John, (later the 5th titular Duke of Perth), were two of the seven persons who engaged themselves to take arms to restore the Stuart family, provided the King of France sent supporting troops. This was a secret group, the Association of Highland

Gentlemen, known as the Concert. In 1745 when Charles Edward Stuart, son of the Old Pretender, landed without French troops, indeed without any troops, the Duke was among the foremost to join him. He, "in an evil hour, was induced to join, with all the forces he could raise, and, by his influence and power, was of essential consequence and service to Charles."

Throughout the campaign with its battles, sieges and marches there is no discrepancy of what happened to him until the rout at Culloden. Wounded in the head and hands he fled away on horseback and was seen late in the day at a considerable distance from the battlefield. Later he may have been hidden by friends and, or, he may have survived in the woods of Drummond Castle. The report of his death was propagated by his friends and encouraged by himself, and there is evidence given by Mrs Jane Hamilton and Mrs Anne Atkinson about this stratagem which developed into leaving Scotland, landing at South Shields, travelling on to Sunderland and up the Wear to the safety of Biddick.

The preparers of the Claim seized on the factual entry about the Duke at Biddick in Parson and White's Directory: "If there was no other evidence, it is presumed that this would, in the eyes of reason and justice, and, it is to be hoped, in a Court of Law, be deemed ample and sufficient proof that the James Drummond who fled from Culloden, and the James Drummond who settled at Biddick were one and the same person, and that this at once refutes all the stories about his alleged death on board ship."

This shows the authoritative standing of such publications at the time, but surely no lawyer would have viewed it as proof.

The 1828 Claim - the Lord John letter

The Claim then mentions, with far less animation, indeed with none, primary evidence come to hand which was far more important, actual proof that it was indeed the Duke of Perth at Biddick: that is the letter to the Duke at Biddick from the his younger brother, Lord John, in Boulogne, dated 16 April 1747, which says:

"I think you had better come to France, and you would be out of danger, as I find you are living in obscurity at Houghton-le-Spring ... you say it is reported that you died on your passage to France."

The Claim says that it was now clear that the opinion that the Duke spent some time in France after Culloden was erroneous. This crucial letter - over eighty years old - was presented in evidence. One would have expected its discovery to be trumpeted with explanation of how it was found and its condition.

The Claim says a strong motive for staying with John Armstrong was that in the event of danger Drummond could be hidden "down a coal mine, a hundred fathoms, perhaps, or more, into the bowels of the earth, and his pursuers might almost as well attempt to enter the infernal regions."

It seems that the Lambtons were the first people to realise who this stranger in the Armstrong habitation could be. That is initially Nicholas Lambton, "a gentlemen of large fortune and possessions." He would be in his mid-fifties when Drummond appeared. Most of his human possessions - his many daughters - had died in their youth. One, Mary, survived, and like her father, lived to her mid-eighties. Nicholas Lambton and the Duke, if such he was, would have to be careful. Drummond would not have to say or imply enough, or let enough be believed, to put himself at Lambton's mercy, causing Lambton to think ofreporting him, and to consider his own position if there was a chance of being accused of knowingly harbouring a traitor. Help, if any, would have to be unexceptional - the ferryboat job could have looked appropriate.

The 1828 Claim - the Lambton family

Had Drummond been influenced in choosing Biddick because of the possibility of sympathy from the Lambtons?

Although the Lambton family had not been courtiers to the Stuarts, as the Drummonds had, they had paid extreme dues to the royal family during the Civil War. Sir William Lambton, knighted when he was twenty-five, after commanding the newly raised Durham troop of dragoons, was slain in 1644 at Marston Moor in that bloody mid-evening rout of the Royalists who were attacked when they thought it was too late in the day for great battle. He was fifty-four. The previous year his twenty-five year old eldest child of his second marriage, also called William, a captain of horse, had been killed at Wakefield.

Also in 1643 John Lambton, nearly twenty-one, from the Lambtons of

Tribley branch, just further west from Lambton, near to Birtley, was slain in Bradford when his Royalist force disdained to surrender and was overpowered. Yorkshire was an unlucky county for the Lambtons. They lost land and fortune for their part in the civil war and some of their collieries were deliberately wrecked and flooded. By the time James II was deposed in 1688 their allegiance to the Stuart dynasty had cooled.

The Claim says that Mary Lambton well knew the history of Drummond and that she was generous in her assistance to the family. She would be about seventeen when Drummond arrived, and about twenty when Drummond and Elizabeth Armstrong married, and it seems that she was drawn to the younger woman.

The phrasing the two daughters said that Major-General Lambton used when he called their father, 'the rebel Drummond', is that of a loyal English soldier. Sir Walter Scott said that in Scotland for forty or fifty years after the Forty-five, 'out' was used rather than 'rebel.' He came 'out.' He was 'out.' The general, three years older than the Biddick Duke, could well have despised him, and he went on to say that he would have him beheaded. The Claim says that this is additional proof that the general was aware of Drummond's status, one which merited decapitation not hanging.

Why didn't General Lambton turn him in? He would have, surely, if he had been certain. It makes one wonder why the Biddick Duke did not assume another name from the start. This is what the Scottish pitmen did who had come to Harraton. Gavin Purdon who wrote the booklet 'Cotia Pit, said it was believed locally that this was why there were so many people in the area called Scott.

In Thomas the claimant's time, seventy years on, was General Lambton's grandson, John George, the 1st Earl of Durham, Radical Jack. Rich because of his collieries, a vehement political figure in a turbulent scene, his young family cursed by the clutches of consumption more deadly than those of the Lambton Worm, and with a short temper he exacerbated by neuralgia, so upsetting that he was excluded from some Cabinet meetings; even he, it was said, assisted Thomas until his limited patience snapped.

Scottish pitmen sometimes escaped from their servitude, worse than that of some slaves, to the relative freedom of working in English pits, and Harraton Colliery, owned by the Lambtons, was a favourite choice. So many runaway Scots worked there that the pit and the hamlet nearby became known as Nova

Scotia, shortened to 'Cotia. This could have been regarded by the Duke as either a proved escape hole for Scots, or a dangerous one for him. He was hiding from vengeful Hanoverians including many Scots, and there might be the odd embittered one at Biddick who would think of betrayal. Perhaps, an ill man, he was taken there. However there is no record of old acquaintances or servants calling to see him.

The Claim purports to talk away the Biddick Duke's acquiescence in his eldest son, James, becoming a pitman. There was expressed opinion that if the Biddick Duke was the person he was represented to be, it is doubtful if he would have allowed his eldest son and heir to work down a pit.

The 1828 Claim - the loss of the evidence

The Claim says that William Drummond, the second son, actually talked to Baron Perth in Scotland. William's unfortunate death was an atrocity itself. His vessel was run down carelessly, and so that no evidence could be heard the master of the offending ship had the clinging survivors beaten off the sides of his vessel and left to drown. One of the crew of his ship later told the story. Unfortunately William had been carrying many of the family papers when the ship went down.

Anne Atkinson, the Duke's eldest child, seventy-eight, provided valuable testimony. "Though," the Claim says, "her early days must have been passed among persons in the lower ranks of society, yet her manners and deportment shew that she must have had intercourse with some higher order, and this is to be traced to the example she had in the superior manners and demeanour of her father."

The same remarks, it was said, were applicable to Elizabeth Peters, now sixty-four. who also provided testimony.

In the 1771 floods their lives and the lives of others were saved by the ferryboat. The two sisters told of the box or chest which held most of the family papers, including the Ducal Patent of Nobility, being swept away. And more papers were lost when William was drowned. (But the crucial letter to the Duke from his younger brother Lord John in France must have survived!)

The 1828 Claim - the Biddick Duke's visit to Scotland

When the Duke travelled to his castle and his estates when they were still annexed by the government, it was said that as he was fearful of being apprehended, his wife went to Newcastle and bought him an old red coat, or soldier's coat, and that he travelled as an old beggar-man.

Why so fearful?

Why leave the journey so late in life?

No one was looking for him. He was as dead to the world outside. The only chance of recognition would be in the vicinity of Drummond Castle. He said he was recognised there by one or two tenants, who were thrilled and sympathetic. But, no doubt, there was danger there. During the Forty-five the Duke had been a soldier of renowned courage: now his behaviour was in contrast with that of Prince Charles Edward, known to be very much alive and continually spied upon. The Prince, much earlier, in 1750, spent six days in London, risking disclosure as he met people and checked on what support there was left for him, and even surveyed the defences of the Tower with an assailant's eye.

On the Biddick Duke's return from Perthshire he told his family a little anecdote which I think has the ring of credibility. A Mr Graeme, a gentleman in whom he could confide, made him take off the old red coat and put on another, and a lady present, who also knew him from the past, exclaimed, "The Duke looks like himself now."

The 1828 Claim - the proofs

There was evidence in the Claim from a William Mackintosh, taken from the testimony of his grandfather, Alexander Mackintosh, of the Duke's wounds at Culloden. The grandfather was with one of the Jacobite forces which missed the battle, and his party was marching towards Culloden when men fleeing from the fighting appeared. The Duke of Perth was on horseback and bleeding from wounds to his face and hands. The Biddick Duke's daughters said the wound to their father's right hand was a very bad one, a deep cut on the back from the wrist to the middle finger which eventually left the finger shorter. The Biddick Duke told them that part of the bone had been taken out.

Only two authorities were cited as saying that the Duke died on shipboard: Douglas's Peerage of Scotland and Dr David Malcolm's Genealogical Memoir of the House of Drummond, and they gave slightly different dates in 1746: 11th May and 13th May. Although the Claim does not mention it, there is not unanimity over which of the two rescuing privateers: La Bellone and Le Mars, took the Duke as a passenger.

Dr Malcolm appears to have been engaged by the Baroness of Perth to write the family history, and the Claim not only discredits his evidence, but presents him as a witness for Thomas, saying, "The hand that administered the poison, has furnished the antidote." On oath the Reverend David Malcolm now stated that he had written from manuscripts laid before him by the late baroness who requested him to bring the memoir down to the present time. He admitted that saying that the late James Drummond, commonly called the Duke of Perth, died at sea on 13th May 1746, was not in accord with the general reports in the district of Perth, which were that the Duke survived and in his old age visited the forfeited estates disguised as a beggar and had been recognised by former tenants.

This secret return was well known in the district of Strathern, Dr Malcolm stated. But the tenants who saw him must now be dead, and it could be difficult to get anyone to swear that they heard their parents or others talk of seeing him, for fear of offending Lord and Lady Gwydyr who were in possession of the estates and were kind and liked.

The Claim comments that recollecting Dr Malcolm's garb it was painful to think that he should publish as a fact that which he disbelieved, and that it was not to be wondered at that the baroness should be desirous of throwing a veil over some happenings.

The dates are revealing. The genealogical memoir written at the behest of the family was published in 1808, some two years after the 1806 meeting with the "poor destitute female relatives." The seeming proof of the Duke's death in 1746 meant that the people from and in County Durham were not who they believed or pretended they were.

The 1828 Claim - the escape from Culloden

The Claim, ready to peck up crumb-like evidence, says that the Attainder Act of

1746 which linked the two brothers, stated that they "on or before the 18th Day of April in the year 1746, did, in a traitorous and hostile Manner, take up Arms, and levy War against his Most Gracious Majesty, within this Realm ... and if they "shall not render themselves to one of his Majesty's Justices of the Peace on or before the 12th Day of July, in the year 1746," then they stand to be adjudged attainted of High Treason, "and shall suffer and forfeit as a Person attainted of High Treason by the Laws of the Land ought to suffer and forfeit."

In what it terms "a strong argument," the Claim says that the act was passed on 4th June, after witnesses had been examined to prove the guilt of the brothers, and the assumption in the wording, after such interrogation, that the Duke was still alive, is further indication that he was, as his death, if it had occurred in May must have been well known to the Government.

This may seem a valid contributory point, but on investigation it loses its edge. The voyages home of La Bellone and Le Mars take rank among the worst ever between Britain and France. On the day they were to leave Loch nan Uamh, with escaping Jacobite officers aboard, including, it is said, the Duke of Perth and Lord John, a British naval group of a twenty-gun ship, the Greyhound, and two sloops, the Baltimore and the Terror, although inferior in gun power to the two large French privateers, sailed into the sea loch to give battle, a battle which was to be, according to John S Gibson in Ships of the '45, the last one of the Forty-five. Le Mars was caught at anchor and took raking broadsides from the Greyhound.

Although French casualties were higher, their heavier guns smashed the sails and rigging of the British ships. Neither side was able to board the other, and after six hours, with their manoeuvrability uncertain, the British withdrew. Despite their damage, especially to Le Mars, the French commanders knew they had to get out of the loch, and hurriedly taking on board the remainder of the Jacobites, who had watched from hillsides the battle and its crucial outcome, they left in the early hours of the following day, 4th May. They dropped their dead into the loch whose waters deposited them on the shoreline. The British dropped their dead when they felt the swell of the Atlantic round Ardnamurchan Point.

The weather was bad, and winds were contrary for the French. Sixty-seven men died of fever on La Bellone, and on Le Mars nearly all the eighty-five badly wounded men died, many had suffered amputations. Although the French were unmolested by more British ships the voyage round Ireland back to the home port of Nantes, gained on 27th May, took twenty-three miserable days. There would not have been time for news of a reported death of the Duke of Perth to have reached London to affect the wording of the Attainder Act passed on 4th June. (In 1747 La Bellone was captured by Rodney, and, lazily renamed The Bellona, entered British service.)

The 1828 Claim - the Charles Edward Drummond bid

Pressing every point the Claim then argued that the grant of the estate in 1785 to the late Captain James Drummond was made on a false assumption, and the king may, by virtue of his prerogative, repeal the grant and declare that the estate be restored to the heir of the former owner.

It then tells of the attempt of Count Melfort, titular Duke, Charles Edward Drummond, who said he was the heir male and chief representative of the House of Drummond, to take over the estates which he also believed had been wrongly assigned to the Honourable Captain James Drummond.

The Count, thought to be a Roman Catholic priest, was, or became, Prelate in the household of the Pope, called upon Elizabeth Peters, the Duke's second daughter, introducing himself as her cousin and asking if she had any documents which would assist him, as the nearest male heir, to obtain his due. He would gratefully reward her. He was shocked to hear that the Duke of Perth had sons, and more, that the first of them, James, Elizabeth's brother, was alive and that he had sons.

"The Count stood amazed at this intelligence ... then took his leave, evidently chagrined and disappointed."

If the meeting was at Biddick it is odd that he did not speak to James. What is pertinent here is that the Count believed that the Duke had not been drowned in 1746 but had lived on in County Durham. This knowledge must have come to him fairly late as in a twenty-eight octavo page pamphlet, The Destruction of Infamy, dated 1816, he wrote that the Duke had died on shipboard in 1746.

How on earth did the Count hear of the family at Biddick? Only, I assume, from people in Perthshire who could recall the old Duke's visit, or from Dr Malcolm.

The Count said that Captain James Drummond was an impostor, and that the real Captain Lord James Drummond, his health ruined after being stabbed by ruffians in Edinburgh, had died at Lisbon when on his way to the East Indies with the second battalion of the 42nd Highlanders: on 13 August 1780, when he was thirty-five. The present incumbent had been an ensign in the East Indies. His uncle, a member of Parliament, had the use of Drummond Castle during its annexation and had the opportunity of possessing himself of material papers.

The Count said that his own claim would have been made in 1785 but for his living in seclusion in France. In 1828 when Thomas Drummond's claim was being prepared it was thought that the Count had been bought off by the holders of the estates who had granted him a yearly stipend of £97. Despite this, he petitioned yet again for the estates in 1838 when he was eighty-six. Although the Claim does not mention this, the Count was in the accepted line for the title, being 5th titular Duke of Melfort and thirteenth titular Earl of Perth, and as he did not die until 1840 he was the person from whom Thomas Drummond would have to divest of the title (although not the estates).

The 1828 Claim - the delays in making the Claim

Near its end the Claim explained that James, the Duke's eldest son, failed to apply in 1785 because he was out of reach of knowledge of what was passing in the world, and that within the family there had been a belief that the estates had become the property of the king who would dispose of them as he pleased. James, too, had a feeling that his life and that of his family could be in jeopardy should it be known that he was the son of a traitor, and that he was actually claiming that he should have what belonged to his father before that treason.

His sisters, however, could not remain suppressed. Mrs Peters said that at their meeting with Lady Perth and her daughter in 1806, the two ladies did not deny their kinship with them. The meeting was in London!

What were the sisters doing in London? The letter by Advocatus Legis, in the previous chapter, mentioned that the approach was made under peculiar circumstances. And the metaphorical door of compassion which he said was closed was a real one, as at a subsequent meeting, when Mrs Peters sent up her name, she was told that the ladies were, "Not at home." Mrs Peters and company would have travelled a long way in pre-railway times, at some expense. They were not rewarded with so much as a conveyed invitation to take rest and refreshment in the servants' quarters!

It was considered that the case of Biddick Claimant Thomas Drummond, born 3rd April 1792, baptised at Penshaw 17th June, was irresistible and could be defeated only if there was proof that the Duke had actually died on board ship in May 1746. Providing such proof was regarded as nearly an absolute impossibility.

The Claim ended by asserting that unless the James Drummond who settled in Biddick was an impostor, there was no doubt that he was the legal lineal heir male; and there had never been any suspicion or imputation that he was an impostor.

A bracketed note says that the proofs and evidence remained in manuscript. How unfortunate that they never reached public print.

Chapter 4
The Presumptuous Summons

"The Case" to the House of Lords 1830

For a presentation to the House of Lords a greatly shortened version of the Claim, called "The Case", was printed - five sheets including a pedigree and a schedule of evidence.

It stated that the restoring Act of 1784 said that the male heir of Lord John, who had died in 1747, was the person to whom it was intended to restore the estate, when he could be ascertained. But later there had been a profound change in the succession, from Male Investiture to Fee Simple Inheritance, the succession now going to heirs and assigns. This meant that when Captain James Drummond, later Lord Perth, to whom the estate was restored in 1785, died in 1800 without male issue, the estate could and did become vested in his daughter.

Following the assumed failure of all male issue from the 1st Duke of Perth, Captain Drummond, claiming that he was the great grandson and nearest male heir of the Earl of Melfort, brother of the 1st Duke of Perth, and of untainted branch, petitioned the king in order to take up the titles, but the petition, referred to the House of Lords, was not pressed as the captain was created an English peer with the title of Lord Perth. The Case imputed that his abandonment of the claim was due to the impossibility of his proving the early death of the 3rd Duke of Perth.

The Case said that the fact that the 3rd Duke did not die aboard ship on 11th May 1746 was proved by the original letter, produced in evidence, written by Lord John Drummond, the Duke's younger brother, in Boulogne, in April 1747, and conveyed by hand to the Duke at Biddick.

Lord John, the Case said, never used the Perth titles because he knew his brother was alive. On Lord John's death, of fever in Antwerp in September 1747, the title went to his eldest uncle, John, who although not affected by the attainders, did not claim the estates. He died in 1756. His half brother, Edward, who succeeded him also made no claim. His death in Paris in 1760, without issue, ended the male line of the 1st Duke of Perth, and opened the right of succession to the heirs of that 1st Duke's brother, the Earl of Melfort.

The Case said that Biddick, as a destination, was probably chosen by the 3rd Duke's confidential friends who helped him in his escape. Quite how long it was after the battle of Culloden was not known, although it must have been a considerable time prior to his brother's letter of 16th April 1747 as it was obvious there had been earlier communication between the two.

That the Duke and the James Drummond who settled at Biddick was the same person was sustained by documentary evidence, and by the testimony of witnesses that he visited his castle and estates disguised as an old beggar man.

He married Elizabeth Armstrong on 6th November 1749. He died in June 1782 aged sixty-nine. James, his eldest son, was baptised 9th August 1752; married Margaret Pearson 2nd April 1776 and died 7th February 1823. His son and heir, Thomas, the claimant, born 3rd April 1792, was the great-great grandson and next lawful heir of the 1st Duke of Perth.

The Biddick Duke's death came two years before the passing of the Act to restore his estates, but even if he had been living he could not have applied for them because of his attainder. On the "supineness" of the eldest son, James, it was explained that the family learned only by chance that the estates had gone to someone else, and, at the time, anyway, they considered them lost because of their father's treason.

"The Case" - the evidence

The schedule of evidence lists what appears to prove Biddick Claimant Thomas Drummond's case: that is, the 1747 letter from Lord John.

So this crucial letter had escaped both being carried away in the floods of 1771 and being in William's care when he was cruelly drowned, as well as the many dangers which any document in a small home has to survive in the course of over eighty years. Depositions of notaries and public functionaries in the Netherlands and France supported its genuineness by a comparison of Lord John's handwriting on papers in public offices in Antwerp, Brussels and Paris.

There were also depositions of the Countess de Genlis and "other persons of high consideration in France" to prove that it was always known there that the 3rd Duke had found asylum in England, and resided there in obscurity for his better concealment, and that the late Prince Charles had often made mention of it.

"The Case" presented

Thomas Drummond's petition, dated 27th March 1830, to King George IV was by royal command presented to the House of Lords by the Earl of Shaftesbury. The Clerk read out a curtailed version of the Case, ending "Wherefore Your Petitioner humbly prays, That Your Majesty will be graciously pleased to declare the said Titles and Dignities to belong to Your Petitioner; or that Your Majesty will be graciously pleased to refer this Petition to the House of Lords, that Your Petitioner may prove before their Lordships his Descent, and Right to the same accordingly."

On 15th April a notice signed by Robert Peel said that the king had referred the petition to The Right Honourable The House of Peers to examine the allegations and to inform His Majesty how they appeared to their Lordships. It was then referred to the Lords Committee of Privileges where after consideration and the hearing of such persons as the committee thought fit they were to report their Opinion to the House.

And there the initial 1830 effort seems to have stopped. No opinion, it seems, was reported to the House. The House of Lords Record Office told me that no reference could be found to the case in the indexes to the minutes of the Committee for Privileges in the 1830s. There was also no follow-up in the local newspapers.

The Canongate Announcement

In the following year, the petition, dated 12th February 1831, was re-presented to the House of Lords, this time by Lord Melbourne, by command of the new king, William IV. It was referred to the House on 22nd February, and the Committee for Privileges was ordered to consider the claim on 5th May or on some other convenient day, "the Petitioner's printed Case having been laid upon their Lordships Table," where it was ordered to lie. Extra printed copies were despatched to several of the lords.

On 25th May, the petition was directed by the Chancery to the Canongate Court House in Edinburgh. Public interest was now such that the birth of a daughter to Mrs Drummond, "wife of the pitman claimant to the Earldom of Perth," on 26th May 1831, was reported in North-east newspapers. This child, Annabella, at least the fifth to Thomas and Jane, died in the following September, the first of eight of their children to die while the parents were alive.

The inquiry, or inquest as it was called, took place on 20th June. An agent appeared for Thomas Drummond before a "respectable" jury of fifteen men of Edinburgh, one of them from the Chancery office there. They examined all the documents, there was no objection to the claim, and their verdict was that the points of the brieve and claim were proven by the depositions of witnesses.

Thomas Drummond, the Biddick Claimant, was unanimously served nearest and lawful heir male to his deceased great grand uncle, Lord Edward Drummond, who had been the last surviving son of James, the 1st Jacobite Duke of Perth.

The drunken heir

Tales of Thomas Drummond indulging in drink as the prospect of titles and riches went to his head are usually placed after the 1831 Canongate announcement.

It was said that he was drunk when summoned to appear before Lord Durham (John George Lambton) on the eve of his appearance at the bar of the House of Lords. Thomas would be in strange and awesome surroundings in London. One account says that it was Lord Durham's butler who got him drunk. At the sight the hard-working, fiery-tempered Durham, an abrasive member of the Cabinet, lost his sympathy and interest.

Although Lord Durham's interest is dwelt upon by local historians, I have seen no mention of it in contemporary newspapers, or in biographical writing on the Earl - he was raised to an Earldom in 1833. I would have expected that the lawyers when appealing for subscriptions would have mentioned such illustrious support. The period was not the most opportune to gain Durham's attention. He was immersed in the preparation of the Reform Bill - passed in 1832 - and within two years his son, three daughters and his mother died.

Fred Hill, the Washington teacher, whose brave lone voice eventually spread concern about the fate of Washington Hall and saved that building from terminal decay or even deliberate demolition, wrote that Thomas enjoyed entertaining in pubs, playing the fiddle and singing and telling stories, and that with the company often paying, he drank too much. Once, parading in his finery, in his dress suit, he provoked derision, and mickey-takers pulled at and tore his swallow-tailed coat. A sad scene.

So, with the winning post seemingly in sight the effort collapsed. The lawyers had been critical earlier of Thomas, but one of them, John Rawling Wilson, of 113, The Side, Newcastle, said later that at that time they had not enough money to carry things forward. Nearly three years were to pass before the spirit reappeared, supported this time with more money, some of it on loan.

A fresh start - 1834

The restart began well. A brieve from the Chancery dated 11th February 1834 for serving Thomas nearest and lawful heir male of Lord John Drummond, his grand uncle, brought the claim back to Canongate Court on 3rd March. An agent appeared again for him before the inquest of another fifteen Edinburgh men.

There were some fresh depositions of witnesses to supplement those of 1831, all gathered by Rawling Wilson, with help from Henry Ingledew. The claim was again found proven, with no person appearing in court to object.

The final step, to claim possession of the estates followed, and immediately, on 5th March, a Summons of Reduction, Declarator, etc was signeted in the Court of Session in Edinburgh. (Reduction meant an action to bring back to or from a state or condition; a restoration; and Declarator an action in which something is prayed to be declared judicially.) That this document was prepared in advance of the second Canongate verdict shows the confidence of the lawyers.

Newcastle newspapers commented that the long-dormant claim was now to be brought to decision; that the right of the claimant was manifest; that the family had been deprived of an inheritance for a political offence for which the present generation could not be accountable - it had been that of forbears long since laid in their graves.

In April the newspapers carried appeals for further subscriptions. The action, expected to be heard early in May, was against the Right Honourable Clementina Sarah Drummond, who was Lady Willoughby de Eresby, and her husband, Peter Robert, Lord Willoughby de Eresby, to recover the possession of the great estates forfeited by Thomas Drummond's grandfather, and erroneously restored in 1785 to Lady Willoughby's father. The local banking houses of Sir M W Ridley and of Backhouse would receive subscriptions, as would three firms of solicitors including the long-serving Henry Ingledew of Dean Street, Newcastle. The Biddick Claimant assured subscribers that in the event of Success he would in gratitude and honour hold himself bound to repay them with interest.

"The Summons" - 1834

A transcription of the long, repetitious Summons, appeared in the Newcastle Journal of 19th April 1834. Printed in full it makes no deference to readability.

William IV lawfully summoned, warned and charged Lady Willoughby de Eresby as pretending right to the lands, lordships, baronies, fisheries, tithes, patronages and other heritages and estates of the Earldom of Perth, and her husband for his own right and interest, and an Edinburgh accountant, Charles Selkrig, a trustee, all to appear before His Majesty's Lords of Council and Session, to answer at the instance of Thomas Drummond of Biddick, in the county palatine of Durham, grandson and heir male of the deceased James Drummond of Perth, known as the Duke of Perth, and heir male to the deceased Edward Drummond, his great grand uncle, also nearest and lawful heir male to his grand uncle, Lord John Drummond, and as such Thomas Drummond had good and undoubted right to prosecute and pursue the action.

Their pretended rights and writings should be exhibited. These were mainly of 1785 when Captain Drummond of the 42nd Regiment of Foot was accepted as the nearest collateral heir of Lord John Drummond. There were also those of 1800 making over lands and estates in favour of his daughter, Clementina Sarah.

The royal summons said that all was to be reduced, retreated, rescinded, cassed, annulled, decerned and declared to have been from the beginning, and to be now, and in all time coming null and void, and of no avail, force, strength or effect, as the decree of 1785 was erroneously obtained by Captain Drummond, that it and other dispositions and writings proceeded upon false grounds, that the captain was not in any respect whatsoever nearest collateral heir male of Lord John Drummond.

The true collateral heir male had been the now deceased James Drummond, the father of Thomas, the present pursuer, and the eldest son of the James Drummond, known as the Duke of Perth, and he had undoubted right to the whole lands, lordships, etc., and also to recover the income from the estate from the year 1785. Lady Willoughby and her husband should remove from the estate at the next lawful term, and discharge and renounce in favour of Thomas Drummond all their pretended rights, and also render just reckoning for rents for each year they had possessed the lands, and make the appropriate payment. Also they should pay to the pursuer £1,000, or some modified sum, to meet the subsequent expenses of his claim.

This was a sweepingly confident case, pushed arrogantly and ruthlessly. Its success would leave the defendants ignominiously beaten and ruined. It was evident that they were to pay for their imperious behaviour towards the Drummond sisters - this was Elizabeth's revenge.

Resisting the temptation to inflict extreme damage on the defendants, apparently reeling on to the ropes, could well have been prudent. It was drawn up by a new name, Ephraim Lockhart, Writer to the Signet, designated as agent; Mr Bruce, clerk, and Henry Ingledew.

The defendants were in serious trouble, actually having to wage legal battle to hold on to the privileged life which had been theirs for years.

The hearing opened in June.

Chapter 5
A parallel story

The crucial letter

If the letter to the Duke, from his brother, Lord John Drummond, in 1747 was genuine then the man was the Duke. If it was a forgery, a concoction, and should there be suspicion of this, then the whole of Thomas Drummond's claim could, probably would, crumble.

But how would a lawyer, or some one else, forge such a letter, or have it forged? He would need an example of Lord John's hand. Was there such in the few family papers remaining? The forgery would have to be good enough to withstand the comparison with Lord John's handwriting on documents in the Netherlands and France. And the paper used would have to appear to be, or be, foreign, and worn, and crinkled, and with the writing faded, and look as if it had been kept for more than eighty years.

How, in 1830 or so, do you obtain writing paper which could have been used in Boulogne in 1747? Would it be worth going to all that time-taking bother and expense, with the probability of disastrous consequences if the deception were found out?

I am surprised that the letter was not written in French. Lord John was more a Frenchman than a Scot. Another reason for him not to have used English was privacy. Of Lord John's letters printed in the Jacobite Epilogue, those to the king, James III are in English, but this was what James expected. Was he not the rightful king of England? He made a point of showing his Englishness, proclaiming his liking for roast beef and his natural preference for ale over the French wines his courtiers sipped. Letters in the book from Lord John to two other correspondents are in French. The presentation documents of Thomas Drummond's claim seem to be written confidently in good faith. This does not preclude such a letter being deceptively written prior to, or in the early days of, the lawyers coming onto the scene.

The possession of the letter and other family documents is not mentioned when the claim was made known to the public in 1826. Then the list of proofs discovered and obtained by Fitz Strathern, the law genealogist, are of dates of baptism, marriage, succession and death, and more such certificates were promised.

The testimony of the Duke's surviving daughter, Mrs Elizabeth Peters, the claimant's aunt, was looked upon as crucial. She was the person who would prove the identity of her father, and her willingness to go north to Scotland to do this was praised. Fitz Strathern went as far as to say that should Mrs Peters die prior to her father's identity being proved, then her nephew would never be preferred to the titles.

In 1826 it seems that Fitz Strathern knew nothing of the 1747 letter. And Thomas Drummond, the claimant, in the letter to the press under his own name in September 1826, does not mention it. Obviously he knew nothing of it as he says then that his grandfather escaped to France in 1746 where he remained for two or three years The first mention of Drummond family papers, including the letter, is in the Claim compiled in late 1828.

The Wensleydale Duke of Perth

There is a parallel extension to the Duke of Perth story, and I'm uncertain whether or not it strengthens or weakens the claim of the man at Biddick. At first hearing it probably appears to weaken it. It is that the Duke of Perth concealed himself not in the lower Wear valley, but in Wensleydale.

The story has not such a hold as the Biddick one, but it is there. H. Speight in his history, Romantic Richmondshire says the 3rd Duke of Perth after Culloden fled from Scotland and secreted himself in Bishopdale, married locally and settled in the dale. (Bishopdale Beck runs into Wensleydale's River Ure a mile or so from Aysgarth.) The Earl's son was for many years parish clerk, and his grandson, a schoolmaster, established a school near Aysgarth Bridge known as the Yore Mills Academy. A man of many talents he was a mathematician of some repute, a land surveyor and an artist and engraver.

In The Striding Dales, Halliwell Sutcliffe, a post-Jacobite romantic who wrote lyrically about the Yorkshire Dales, tells of reminiscing with a Wharfedale farmer. He said he was a descendant of the 3rd Duke of Perth, who when unwell during the retreat from Derby had lain up for two days at a farm in the dale. (Wharfedale is three or four miles over the hills from the top end of Bishopdale.) And that, after Culloden the Duke, evading the searching soldiers as he headed south, crossed the Solway into Cumberland and made the hospitable Wharfedale farm his objective.

There, helped by the caring attention of the farmer's daughter, Nut-brown Nell, he recovered his health, married Nell and stayed on doing farm work. The Wharfedale farmer told Sutcliffe that there was a Drummond still living in Aysgarth in Wensleydale. Sutcliffe later met this man, an old schoolmaster, John Drummond, who said he was the great grandson of the Duke, and that the hospitable farm had not been in Wharfedale, but in the Aysgarth area, which could be Bishopdale. I think "great grandson" is assuming a too-near proximity. Sutcliffe was writing of the 1920s. Taking guidance from the Drummonds of Biddick, the great grand children of the Duke were being born in the 1820s.

The 1745 Campaign

If the Duke had received kindness at the farm, this was probably exceptional and so was memorable. The retreating Jacobites were harried by the people they passed through as much as the people dared. Stragglers, often sick, were ill treated, sometimes killed.

But what was the Duke doing in those Yorkshire dales? Four thousand men on the march, often spread themselves a little, but they had to keep in touch. And they retreated over the same terrain they had advanced, the flat land west of the Pennines. They were in the hills when they had no choice, mainly between Penrith and Kendal going over Shap. They had cannon to haul, and a baggage train. They went to and from Derby via Preston, Wigan, Manchester, and Macclesfield.

A clansman adrift by himself at the top of Wharfedale or in deep and little-known Bishopdale would probably be a deserter. The Duke was one of the elite. A member of the Prince's war counsel. At first he was lieutenant-general, sharing overall command with Lord George Murray. Often he would be on horseback, occasionally in a chaise. He had brought two hundred men with him to join the Prince in 1745, and on 17th September when entering Edinburgh he rode on the right of the Prince with David, Lord Elcho on the left. The Prince's horse was a bay gelding which the Duke had presented to him.

The retreat from Derby had to be orderly because the people had become openly hostile. I do not think it is credible that the Duke, alone and unwell, was adrift from the others in the depths of the Yorkshire dales. This leaves the same question as with the Biddick man. Who was he if he wasn't the Duke? The story seems to be a shadow of the Biddick one, and, on reflection, it could be argued strengthens the main story.

The Duke of Perth was against the retreat. His was one of only two voices supporting the distraught Prince at that momentous early morning meeting in Derby on 5th December 1745. The Prince seems to have been unaware of the growing uneasiness of the clan leaders. Their last battle had been outside Edinburgh at Prestonpans and they were now deep into England and no opposing force had been able to confront them in strength. But their run of success had to continue until they had put the Stuarts back on the throne in London.

They were a small force of 4,500 enclosed in a country which did not want them. Even if they reached London and found that George II had fled, that may not be final victory, far greater forces could assemble and encircle them. Probably once they invaded England on their own, without armed support from France, and found the English uninterested, they were lost souls. They would have had a chance if they had stayed in Scotland, proclaimed the Stuarts there, and broken away from the union with England.

But even in Scotland there were many against the Catholic Stuarts, including some Highland clans. Carolly Erickson in Bonnie Prince Charlie, published in 1993, said the most important clans were loyal to the Hanoverians and fought against the rebels. There was a considerable proportion of Scots in the government army at Culloden. Much of the merciless hounding which followed was the work of Scots. Scottish nationalists or anti-English or anti-union people managed for years to have Culloden distortingly viewed as an England v Scotland battle.

The arguments at Derby to return before they were trapped and all of them killed or captured seemed strong, but once accepted the army's spirit fell. David, Lord Elcho, who was at the crucial confrontation, told of Lord George Murray saying that they had marched into the heart of England ready to join any party that would declare for the Prince, but none had, and no one had sent money, or intelligence, or the least advice. If the Prince could produce any letter from any person of distinction in which there was an invitation for the army to go to London, or to any other part of England, then they were ready to go. The people they had passed through had seemed to be enemies rather than friends. They were a force of only 4500, and they had never thought of putting a king on the English throne by themselves. If they were to evade enemy forces and reach London, even against hostile mobs their numbers would not be great.

At the time the Duke of Cumberland's army was in the Stafford area, as near to London as the Jacobites. General Wade's army was hard-marching down the east, and a third army was being assembled between them and London. Yet, in the face of all that, it is generally thought that the decision to retreat was wrong. If they had had premonition of what was in store for them at Culloden no doubt it was. They'd been led shrewdly by Murray and they might well have got to London without formidable confrontation.

Sir Charles Petrie in The Jacobite Movement wrote, "They looked at the weakness of their position, and entirely ignored its strength." There had been uneasiness among the leaders about invading England from the start. Their interest had been in their own country. They had more to lose than the young headstrong Prince. The logical arguments set forth by Lord George Murray were held grimly enough to resist the stormings and pleadings and threats of the shocked and irate Prince, who, probably rightly, sensed they were on a victory roll. The overwhelming consensus was to abandon the march on London. The Prince, a light heart turned heavy, found a place at the rear. He knew now, that when it mattered, the divine right of Stuart Princes could be as nothing even to those nearest to him. He announced that there would be no more Councils of War; that he would be accountable to no one but his father.

The Wensleydale Duke's case examined

If the Duke of Perth had wandered off by himself during the retreat, this would have been remarked upon in some of the accounts. In fact in country in a line west of Wharfedale and Bishopdale he was in the van of the Jacobite army when he was sent ahead from Lancaster to Kendal. This was where he narrowly escaped death or injury from a lone shot. He became too ill to travel and did stay a short while at a hamlet south of Kendal, but he was well west of hilly Yorkshire. I think we can dismiss that he stayed in a Yorkshire dale during the retreat.

Before the rebellion the Duke frequently visited Yorkshire. He attended York races so often that Horace Walpole described him as 'a foolish horse-racing boy'. His enjoyment of racing was genuine – but York was also a meeting place of English Jacobites.

The Duke once assured the Jacobite agent, James Murray of Broughton, that the mayor and aldermen of York had engaged to raise ten thousand Yorkshiremen in the cause on hearing of a Jacobite invasion in force. Such were the ludicrous expectations.

There was another connection, a romantic one, mentioned by Dr Leo Gooch of Wolsingham in his The Desperate Factions? a rich mine of information on Jacobites of the north. The Duke had offered to marry Cicely Mayes, the only daughter of John Mayes, a wealthy and eminent Catholic lawyer of The Friarage, Yarm, but the lawyer, who had already turned away a succession of suitors, rejected the Duke too. James Murray writing to the Old Pretender's secretary in July 1743 said, "the Duke of P returned from York after having got a very possitive and harsh Refusall from the Lady to whom he was making his addresses".

Cicely Mayes was no Nut-brown Nell.

Chapter 6
The Duke on active service

The Third Duke's mother

When the Duke of Cumberland, chasing the Jacobites, reached Crieff in Perthshire in early February 1746, he wrote that they were now marching through Drummond's estates and he had thought fit to let the soldiers "a little loose," and he had told that "troublesome old woman," the Duchess of Perth at Drummond Castle, to write and tell her son to release all prisoners, otherwise the castle would be burned and destroyed. He sent a subaltern and twenty dragoons to remain with her until she received an answer from her son.

Her retort could well have annoyed him, as on the 11th February, the Duchess and her kinswoman, the Countess of Strathallan, were imprisoned in Edinburgh Castle. They were there until 17th November when they were released on bail.

Cumberland could also have been annoyed that the duchess had had the greater part of the walls of the castle levelled to the foundations to lessen the temptation to have it seized by his troops and used as a garrison. That she had a reputation was shown by the off-the-cuff remark of a Government soldier at the battle of Falkirk when men stepped aside to allow children to run away. A bouncing hare brought up the rear and the soldier commented, 'Hollo, the Duke of Perth's mother". The account in Henry Drummond's Noble British Families says that the duchess was at the castle until it was "destroyed" in 1748 when she retired to Stobhall, the family's old residence, where she lived till she was ninety, dying in 1773.

One would have thought the Biddick Duke would have written to her telling her that he was alive. Would he not have risked a visit to the castle at Stobhall, or to another rendezvous? If he had, or had written, such knowledge could have been retained within a small circle for a considerable time. Surely he must have felt concern over his mother's situation, and wondered how the family was coping The seemingly ludicrous comment from her that she was dissatisfied with him for not participating to more effect in the rebellion, implies a distance in feeling between them, but he was the male head of the family and that had important implications. Even if sympathy had been lost between them, his mother and sister, Lady Mary Drummond, should know that he was alive. It seems inconceivable that he did not communicate.

In 1847, during evidence in support of George Drummond's claim to the title, there is a letter written in 1748 by John, the 3rd Duke's uncle, saying that Lady Mary Drummond had arrived at his house in Perth from London, and that she'd expressed the hope that all his affairs would prosper. The implication is that Lady Mary was at ease with her uncle, had accepted reports of her brother's death and had no knowledge of the man at Biddick.

The invasion plot - 1745

The depth and length of the Duke of Perth's commitment to the Stuart dynasty, and his role in the Forty-five, is not, I think, appreciated.

In 1740 he and his Uncle John were two of seven eminent Scots who secretly pledged that they would fight, that was if there were French troops in support. Early in 1744 a French army was being assembled for an invasion of Britain, but bad weather wrecked many of the ships and the invasion was called off. During this scare the 3rd Duke, knowing he was in danger of being arrested, lay low in a friend's estate to the north in the Balmoral area. Soldiers came to Drummond Castle from Stirling Castle to take him prisoner. His redoubtable mother gave them politic hospitality.

Late in the year at a meeting of the Buck Club, founded by Lord Elcho and Lord George Murray in Edinburgh, he was one of those who said that they would join with Charles in any event, without the six thousand regular troops, arms for ten thousand more and thirty thousand louis d'or which Murray and others stipulated should accompany Charles when he landed. In Christmas week of 1744 the Duke sent an emissary, John Blaw, to the Prince in France - a twenty-four day journey - informing him of the situation in Scotland. Blaw was taken prisoner on his return and spent two and a half years in prison without being charged.

In May 1745, Bonnie Prince Charlie, devastated at the aborted invasion, brooding in seaside rooms in the Pas-de-Calais, broke his frustration by deciding he would land with what little help he could muster. He despatched this shock information with Sir Hector Munro saying that the papers were to be opened in the presence of the Duke of Perth. Before he reached the Duke, Munro, instead of making for a safe house in the country, failed to resist the temptation to spend time in Edinburgh buying footwear. He was noticed and arrested and the papers confiscated. However, prior to his arrest, he had told one or two of the faithful of the contents.

Also in that month a ruse to capture the 3rd Duke nearly succeeded, when a Captain Campbell, a dinner guest at Drummond Castle, asked to have a word with him in another room, where he announced that he had a company of soldiers outside and that the Duke was now his prisoner. The Duke asked permission to speak to his neighbour and main guest who had deceived him by pretending that Campbell was a friendly companion, but when he left the room he slipped through a private door into his own grounds and escaped. Another account was that he went into a closet to put on different clothing, locked the door behind him and left by some backstairs.

The Duke's estates were vast, stretching over forty-six miles. There were leases and enclosures and some good stone houses, and he had tried to achieve a balanced economy At Perth he established a timber factory - destroyed by government forces in 1746, and in Crieff he had a large house built for linen manufacture. With growing families some farmsteads were overcrowded, and in a venture to attract people away it was proposed to establish new towns. The plan for the new town of Callander owned by the Duke is dated 1739. But not all his income was spent on upkeep and improvement. He handed John Murray, the Jacobite secretary, fifteen hundred pounds to give to the Prince, and even spoke of mortgaging his estates for the same purpose. So wealthy, in a position of power, he was doing a very worthwhile job for his country, family, tenants and the many Drummonds, but when Bonnie Prince Charlie himself was on his doorstep there was no hesitation.

The Third Duke's character

At Prestonpans (21st September 1745) the 3rd Duke commanded the van, or right of the line, an honour which he had to alternate with Lord George Murray. The two were called, ironically, the Prince's right and left hand men. Overall command switched each day between them. This was a ludicrous arrangement which was peremptorily broken by an exasperated Lord George after the siege of Carlisle.

At Prestonpans the Jacobites were indebted to a local young man who, because of his snipe shooting, knew of a path through a morass which the Government army had assumed was a sufficient barrier against an advance. During the night the Jacobites made a single-file march and early the next morning Sir John Cope's army awoke to find their enemy lining up to attack their exposed left flank. "Hey, Johnnie Cope, are ye waukin' yet!" Such proximity before the charge was of great matter especially to the MacGregor company, then in the Duke of Perth's regiment. They wielded extra sharpened scythes at the end of long poles which, at a certain swinging distance, was "a most murderous weapon" against man and horse, but at other distances no use at all.

The Duke had brought two hundred of his own men with him, and a present of two hundred guineas. It is naive to imagine that all those two hundred men and youths were there voluntarily. Although no doubt during the campaign an enthusiasm developed, it didn't affect their lives one iota if George II or James III was on the throne. Probably there was a little less chance of near-starvation under the Hanoverian.

Many of the Duke's tenants were Protestants, and the improvements he had brought about on the estates diminished the attraction of being a rebel soldier. In this context Carolly Erickson told of a Dumfries magistrate writing to a friend in Carlisle in mid-September 1745 that the Duke of Perth had shot three of his tenants who had refused to come out for Bonnie Prince Charlie. I'd guess this was malicious rumour, frequent in civil strife. Many Scots at the time were indignant at the, to them, unwarranted upset to their lives which the Prince's fanaticism was bringing about. Presbyterian ministers ranted angrily against the Prince, his house and his followers. To kill men who refused to come out was extreme, but having them beaten was not, nor threatening to burn dwelling roofs and sometimes doing so, and slaughtering tenants' or clansmen's cattle. A chieftain's decision to fight included his clan.

John Prebble in Culloden tells of harsh measures against hesitant or rebellious Gordon, Macdonald and Cameron clansmen. Alexander

MacGrowther, surely at the age of seventy-six the oldest lieutenant in the rebel army, was one of the men left reluctantly by the Duke at Carlisle during the retreat. Maybe MacGrowther himself had had enough of forced marching. At his trial he said that he had been bound with ropes and taken from his home in Glenartney to join the Duke of Perth's regiment. Why should this have been done to an old man? Maybe he was a master of some craft, and worth his weight in gold to a campaigning army. Despite his age and being forced to join he was sentenced to death. To have averted this it seems he should at least have made attempts to desert. He was reprieved because of representations made by the Scandinavian ambassador.

The only behavioural criticism of the Duke I have read is that he spoke too much and too fast. John Murray of Broughton, who became secretary to the Prince, said the Duke was "rather over-tedious in his discourses," had "an over-fondness to speak broad Scots, but had undaunted courage". The Chevalier de Johnstone, for a time aide-de-camp to Lord George Murray, said the Duke was of mild and gentle disposition, was every way honourable, and brave even to excess. Sir Charles Petrie in The Jacobite Movement said the Duke's English was indifferent, but in every sense of the word he was a gentleman.

His character and nature were shown clearly after the fall of Carlisle in November 1745. The Jacobite army was encamped at Brampton and after scouts sent towards Newcastle had reported that General Wade's army was more than thirty miles away and didn't seem to be moving, Murray recommended that Carlisle and its castle be besieged. The castle was defended by the Cumberland and Westmorland militia.

Bonnie Prince Charlie put the 3rd Duke of Perth in command of the siege, and that night trenches were opened between the gates of the castle some little distance from the walls. The Highlanders had no liking for digging, especially in hard ground in cold weather, and to spur them the Duke himself laboured in shirt sleeves. When lightweight cannon were brought up the next day, the apprehensive militiamen lost what little heart they had, and with mutiny spreading, an offer of the capitulation of the town was made. Informed of this by the Duke, the Prince stipulated that capitulation must include the castle. In Edinburgh the castle had not surrendered and had caused a deal of trouble, but at Carlisle, with militiamen deserting, the castle did not hold out.

The capitulation terms were given and signed by the Duke; the mayor and others came to Brampton and on their knees presented the keys of the city to the Prince, then returned to Carlisle in time to welcome him, when, preceded by more than a hundred pipers, he entered, mounted on a white charger.

At Carlisle, Lord George Murray, the most experienced soldier, was ignored as much as possible by the Prince. He was twice the age of the Prince and of haughty disposition, and the Prince found it easier to deal with the Duke of Perth or issue commands through his own secretary. Murray should have been informed of, or even better, consulted over the Prince's suggested capitulation terms, and allowed to conduct the surrender.

Murray was a Protestant, and the promise to the inhabitants of the continued enjoyment of their religion, would have come with better assurance from him than from the Roman Catholic Duke of Perth. A Catholic accepting surrender of an English city could cause general concern. Murray had been writing instructions about the blockading of Carlisle since five that morning, and late in the day, hearing that terms had been agreed, he sent a terse note to the Prince saying that it was evident that his advice carried little weight and he therefore gave up his commission of lieutenant general, but he would continue to serve as a volunteer.

To his brother, the Duke of Atholl, he said he could be of more use charging in the front rank of Atholl men, and that if a hole could not be found for him in the Duke's quarters he would 'lye' with the men in a barn. Charles, whose dislike – even distrust of Murray – was to become obsessional, replied the same night that he accepted Murray's demission as lieutenant general and his future services as a volunteer.

Alarm at the news spread through the Jacobite army, and leaders petitioned Charles to reinstate Murray. The Duke of Perth, now the new single commander, was liked and his loyalty and bravery were beyond doubt, but he had nowhere near Murray's command of strategy, and there was also his Roman Catholicism. He didn't need telling about such things. He arranged a meeting between Charles and Murray, and to ease Murray's reinstatement, said he would resign as lieutenant general and co-commander, and revert to command of his own regiment.

For this tactful and generous act he was to receive admiring words from future historians, and the heartfelt thanks of the army at the time, although there was none from the hurt and haughty Lord George. Compton Mackenzie in his Prince Charlie said the Duke was always magnanimous. Without his magnanimity at Carlisle the army could have disintegrated.

In the retreat, a month later, the Duke exhausted himself helping others to cross the River Esk near Longtown, when the army, after leaving Carlisle, and with Cumberland's army not far behind, was confronted by a swollen river and no bridge. The flowing water was at shoulder height. Later he missed the battle of Falkirk as he was in command of twelve hundred men laying siege to Stirling Castle, in his home country.

He took over the pursuit of Lord Loudon's royal garrison of irregulars at Inverness when they retreated round the Moray and Cromarty Firths to the far side of Dornoch Firth. Thirty-four fishing boats, stealthily assembled at Findhorn, were sailed across the mouth of the Moray Firth at night, evading the patrolling navy, and rounding Tarbat Ness got to Tain on the southern side of Dornoch Firth the following morning. There the Duke and a strong force embarked that night, and arrived out of the fog the next morning near to Dornoch, where the Duke, it was said, was first ashore, jumping into four feet of water. They scattered Loudon's men, capturing some two hundred of them, and four vessels with arms, victuals, uniforms, furniture and money. Not a single shot was fired nor a drop of blood shed, says one account, which sounds like rhetoric. The Dictionary of National Biography rates this raid as the Duke's chief exploit. The bulk of Loudon's men, some nine hundred, fled the mainland to the safety of Skye, away from the fighting altogether. They included Duncan Forbes of Culloden, Lord President of the Court of Session, whose eloquence had dissuaded some clan leaders from joining the rebellion. It was said if Forbes had been a Jacobite, not four thousand but nearly twenty thousand Scots would have marched into England and that James III would have been crowned.

It must have seemed incongruous to Forbes that the Prince had chosen a moor on his estate to wage the crucial battle and his house for headquarters.

Culloden

The Duke was present throughout Culloden, one of many doomed battles of accumulating disaster, wrong from the start, and which are such sorry tales that one is reluctant to embark on the telling of them.

On 16th April 1746 the clans were scattered, the army well below full strength, executive action was now with the starry-eyed and wilful Prince and his close surround of friends. The men were hungry because the commissariat was now incompetent - food baked for them in Inverness had not been brought up, and the field where they would stand for battle, chosen by Quartermaster General O'Sullivan, was a bad choice. Its selection depressed the more knowledgeable.

Lord George Murray had more favourable land across the Moray Firth reconnoitred, but O'Sullivan and the Prince had made up their minds. These factors were probably sufficient to ensure defeat, but an extra decisive one was the exhausting aborted foray, the night before the battle, to encircle Cumberland's army at Nairn.

The plan was the idea of the Prince and his circle of Irish friends, and Murray was 'very sensible of the danger should it miscarry,' - Cumberland's army was some ten miles away - but eventually he spoke up for it, as at least it moved the imminent conflict away from the moor at Culloden. But army stomachs had not been looked after and the night march started late because men were searching for food.

The terrain was difficult in the dark, there was opportunity for young men, wondering what on earth they were doing there, to slip away and begin the trek home. Progress was slow, numbers became fewer, and at two in the morning when they had hoped to launch the attacks they were nowhere near to the positions. There was now no chance of a surprise attack. Lord George Murray's column turned about, and instructions were sent to the Duke of Perth, who was leading the second column, to do the same.

So the Prince, towards the rear of the Duke's column, saw men returning. Angrily he called for the Duke to explain, and the Duke told him that the first line had turned back three-quarters of an hour before. They got back to their inhospitable moor about six or seven in the morning. Some staggered on to Inverness hoping to find food there. Others fell asleep, some to experience only fearful moments of consciousness when the enemy was among them. Sleepy and hungry, others lined up for battle. Afterwards, in his letter to the Prince from Ruthven, Lord George said the army had been starved for three days and that this was the reason for the failure of the night march, when a third of the men scattered to Inverness in search of food and those who marched had not the spirit or the fitness to go at the pace required. Old Lord Lovat said, before his execution, 'None but a mad fool would have fought that day'.

At the battle Murray commanded the right of the front line, the Duke the left, and his brother, Lord John, the centre. The eventual Highland charge, the men desperate under the cannonade, was made by the right. With good fortune and a cool head, Lord George Murray was one of the few officers in that part of the field to survive.

The Duke of Perth had a frustrating time. He could conjure no supporting charge. The Macdonalds were angry at not being in the place of honour on the right, and in addition, once they were clear of a protecting wall on their left, any attempted charge would leave them open to a flank attack. Seizing colours the Duke cried that if they showed their accustomed valour he would change his name from Drummond to Macdonald, but this failed to impress. Later, when he saw the centre and right giving way, he rode through the fire in an attempt to stay the rout, and was wounded in the shoulder. All the Macdonalds did not join in the rout. Some of their leaders, with loyal men round them, dashed forward to what was now useless premature death.

The Jacobite army was not smashed into individuals and small parties. Four foot regiments and two cavalry formations never fired a shot, and many in the second line fired only when covering the retreating front line. These and other survivors, with others who had missed the battle, still made a substantial force, and most of them made their way to Ruthven in Badenoch some fourteen miles distant.

The Prince stayed the first night about twenty miles from Culloden. Some fifteen hundred men, including the Duke of Perth, Lord John and Lord George Murray, assembled in the valley at Ruthven. Whether or not that force could have recovered and grown into a significant army again we will never know. Recovery and growth could have led to further disaster, although such could scarcely be worse than the aftermath of Culloden. At Ruthven the Prince was absent and there were no provisions and no money.

Murray could see no hope, and there he penned his bitter letter to the Prince about recent decisions and incompetence. But before that could have been received, on their second morning at Ruthven, one from the Prince arrived which ended the campaign. It was read out by Murray and Lord John: "Let every man seek his own safety the best way he can."

It was all over. The surviving Jacobite leaders ruined, their lands left open to the vengeance of the royal forces, and themselves wanted for treason.

There is an account of the Duke of Perth and the colonel of the MacGregors - the MacGregors had at first served in the Duke's regiment - parting in tears. The Chevalier Johnstone said, "The Highlanders gave vent to their grief in wild howlings and lamentations; the tears flowed down their cheeks when they thought that their country was now at the discretion of the Duke of Cumberland".

It has been said, shrewdly, that it was after Culloden that Prince Charles, evading his persistent hunters, conquered Scottish hearts. He was an extraordinarily fit young man, still sustained by his arrogant belief in his role, but having to accept reservations. The English had not come forth, but had fought against him, and even many Scots had - all fought against their rightful Prince. Now with the cohesion of the Jacobite army lifted away, he was vulnerable to betrayal. He was the greatest prize. A man could win a pardon and further reward by revealing his whereabouts.

After Culloden

As for the Duke of Perth, that announcement at Ruthven would be the dagger thrust from which there was no recovery. All was now gone: his dreams, his home, his possessions, and he was weak and sickly. A K Smith in his booklet The Noblest Jacobite of All published in 1995, full of information of the Jacobites of old Perthshire, says that at Culloden, the Duke - 'the noblest Jacobite' - was saved by his servants when he was hit on the shoulder on the return half of his hazardous ride along the breaking front line. He makes no mention of hand injury.

If the Duke had been well, surely he, and not Lord John, would have joined with Murray in making known the Prince's capitulation message. Some of those at Ruthven decided to risk surrendering in preference to going into the hills, but the Duke and Lord George Murray were among those who took to the hills. There was a chance of life that way, or of quiet death: surrender could lead only to a violent death.

Lord George Murray considered starting reports of his own death and living under a false name in Poland, not only to make life easier but to facilitate the transfer of his estates to one of his sons. (His eldest son, on the government side in the Forty-five, became the 3rd Duke of Atholl.) After

Ruthven, Lord George turned south, not west, and going through his own Strathallan lands found refuge, it is believed, in the forest of Glenartney in the Perth estate some seven miles from Drummond Castle. He eventually got over to the continent and Poland, but lived mainly at Cleves (Kleve) just over the Rhine into old Prussia, and finally in Holland.

After fourteen years in exile, Murray died there in 1760. He became distant from other Jacobite exiles. Not because of James III, the old Pretender, but because of Prince Charles. In 1745 the Prince had invited Murray to join him - Murray had been pardoned for being out in the Fifteen - and he joined, it was an issue of honour for him. He had joined with no illusions, aware that defeat in the end was more than a possibility. There was a generation of experience dividing them. The Prince's antipathy towards him had grown and now soared beyond his control so that when Murray, prepared to be conciliatory, visited Paris in the summer of 1747 the Prince ordered him not to appear in his presence and to leave the city. To his father he wrote that such a devil should be secured immediately in some castle without liberty of pen or papers. No doubt Lord George wondered why he and others risked so much for such a man.

Immediately after Culloden servants rode at each side of the Duke of Perth to guard him from slipping off his horse. Later, at times, they carried him.

He stayed a night or two at the home of Doctor Archibald Cameron, and spent some days at a shieling of Dr Cameron's high in the hills. Seven years later, Dr Cameron was executed at Tower Hill, the last of the Jacobites to pay the full penalty. He was the brother of Lochiel of Cameron, the clan leader who joined the Prince early, despite misgivings because of the disappointing support.

In the third week after Culloden the Duke was in the hills above the west coast when wonderful news came of the two French ships nearby in Loch nan Uamh, the same place where the Prince had arrived the previous July to spark off the mad adventure and tragedy.

He was borne down to the loch side, and wrapped in a blanket, listening to the plopping of the little waves on the whitish sand, waited for a boat.

Chapter 7
'Dear Mr Daniel...'

The death at sea story

Outside of Biddick the general belief was that the Duke died at sea. Even the Old Pretender, James III to Jacobites, the father of Prince Charles Edward, had been informed of the death. Writing from Rome to his son, "My dearest Carluccio," on 4th July 1746, not knowing if the Prince was alive and if so was free, he said, "For tho' I have heard Lord John, now Duke of Perth, and Sir Thomas (Sheridan) are both come to Paris, I have not yet heard from them, but shall, I suppose, next post". (The Stuart Papers at Windsor.)

A week later, 11th July, he replied to Lord John, "I received by last French post your letter of the 19th June. My own and The Prince's misfortune do not make me less sensible of the loss you have made of your Brother and indeed of that the Cause and ourselves have made in him. Nobody is better acquainted with the merits of your Family than myself, nor does more justice to it ... " (Jacobite Epilogue.) On the day his father was writing this, the Prince was hiding in a wood in Borrodale in Arasaig/Moidart country after eluding his pursuers in the islands, and, a friend just captured, was about to move to a high cave four miles inland.

Would Lord John have informed King James of the death if it was a ploy? He and the Duke were said to be on the same ship, and if in truth his brother was not on it, and he, Lord John, was part of a subterfuge, would he have carried the pretence so far as to give false information to his king?

All Jacobite historians who have mentioned the death of the Duke of Perth say that it happened on shipboard on his way to France. Sir Charles Petrie, thinking of imprisonment, trial and execution, said that perhaps the Duke was lucky to die that way. But I fancy that the Duke would have faced execution bravely, like Lord Balmerino, one of those who surrendered.

The accepted death of the Duke on board ship would be death in misery amid squalor and noise and smells and overcrowding. Lord John and David, Lord Elcho, were also on that voyage, but what is taken by historians as evidence of the Duke's death comes from the writings of an Englishman, Captain John Daniel. (The evidence proffered to and accepted by the Lords Committee of Privileges came from France: an official letter from Nantes to the Minister of Marine in Paris.)

Captain Daniel's manuscript

Captain John Daniel, a Roman Catholic, from the Fylde area of Lancashire, spoke to the Duke of Perth at an inn near Preston during the march south, and when the Duke invited him to join and offered his patronage, he accepted immediately. Daniel was attached to hussars - Elcho's Life Guards and then Balmerino's. He was proud of his friendship with the Duke and had a great liking for him. Henrietta Taylor, in Jacobite Epilogue, says that in May 1746 he was a witness of the death and burial at sea of his noble patron.

Daniel's account of his part in the rebellion was not generally available until 1916 when it was included in Origins of the Forty-five, edited by Walter Biggar Blaikie and printed for the Scottish History Society. When I read that there had existed only two copies of the manuscript, and that one had been preserved at Drummond Castle, I realised that it was likely that this would be to have precious evidence, a first-hand account, of the Duke's death to thwart the claim of the Biddick Claimant Thomas Drummond.

Blaikie says the Drummond Castle manuscript carried a certification from R B Gibson of Exmouth, Devon, dated September 1830, that it was a correct copy of the original and that he, Gibson, had conversed with his late friend Captain Daniel frequently about its contents, particularly about the Duke of Perth's death. The account of Daniel's adventures - A True Account of Mr John Daniel's Progress with Prince Charles - is fifty-seven pages long. The death of the Duke is told briefly in the penultimate paragraph, so its singling out in the certification implies especial interest, and I surmise that this came from the occupants of Drummond Castle, and that they probably commissioned the copying.

This means prior awareness of Daniel's writing. Lady de Eresby would know of Thomas Drummond's petition to the king made Early in 1830, and that after it had been referred to the House of Lords' Committee of Privileges, printed copies of the case had been sent to various noblemen. One would expect a searching for corroboration of the Duke's death in 1746.

Daniel wrote his account in France in a time when he still had no doubts but that the Stuart cause would triumph and that Prince Charles as Charles III would reign in Britain. He could well have returned to England, to the south-west, late in life to a part of the country where he was not known. Gibson must have been considerably younger. Lady de Eresby and her husband, or their solicitors, could well have sought the advice of historians of the Forty-five among whom there was awareness of Daniel's account.

Blaikie says that he saw both manuscripts. The older one was difficult to read and the spelling eccentric. The Drummond Castle script was in modern spelling. Other than the spelling they were practically identical. One can assume if something as important as the death of the Duke was not mentioned in the eighteenth century script, but was added for the later one, that he would have noticed and commented upon it. Blaikie's interest was general.

Captain Daniel's story

Daniel was in his early twenties, twenty-two or a little older. "Serve God and then your King," was his exhortation, but that the king should be a Stuart. In late November 1745 he saw "this loyal army" between Lancaster and Garstang with Prince Charles marching at the head and at the sight his fate was decided. It was sealed a little later when the Duke of Perth entered the public house he was in and asked questions about the attitude of local people.

Daniel joined the army later that day at Garstang. When the army marched on to Preston the Duke put him in charge of forty men and told him to ride round to places he knew proclaiming and recruiting. Young Daniel did this, distributing manifestos and exhorting people to shake off the infamous yoke of tyranny and prove that they remained true English hearts and exert their liberties under a Prince who was come for their sakes. Alas, Daniel wrote, few consented to join. He brought in thirty-nine, which doesn't seem a bad haul to me. The Duke was disappointed but told him that soon there would be a great joining. The fervent hope of the army was that thousands would flock to them in England.

Daniel, who was made a captain in command of a company, said the Duke was the epitome of all that was good, and that it would require the pen of an angel to properly celebrate his merits. His own father, who had suffered in the Fifteen, lived in Preston and told him to act to the best of his power the part of a brave soldier, and to comfort those he found in misery. Daniel tells of an incident at Derby which reveals the fear felt by the invaded. When he reached his requisitioned billet the master of the house and his wife had fled and there was a spread of watches and jewellery on a table. A frightened housekeeper hoped that he would be satisfied with taking them instead of killing or ill-treating the staff.

During the retreat from Derby Daniel's role as a cavalryman meant that he was not among those unfortunates left at Carlisle castle. Members of the month-old, small, and ill-fated, Manchester Regiment were, and there were probably some of those Lancashire lads he had recruited among them. Just under four hundred men were left, more than half were Scots, including, in spite of the Duke of Perth's expressed disagreement, some members of his own regiment, seven of them officers. The proportion of officers was high among the English left at the castle - higher than one in five.

The Prince, it seems, wanted a holding should he return to England, but with two Hanoverian armies with artillery approaching, the garrison had no chance. Murray suggested destroying part of the fortifications and leaving the city so there would be no problem in taking it should they be back, or, he said, come back through Brampton not Carlisle. The Prince is blamed for seemingly treating the Jacobite Carlisle garrison as expendable; for his lax regard of the situation and of the fate of the men. And the army couldn't afford to be so wasteful. Searching for an explanation some people thought at the time that such was the Prince's deep disappointment and disgust with the English, that he had begun to resent even those who had joined him. John Daniel would have drawn his sword at this.

John Prebble observed that it is to be hoped that the Prince did not know what he was doing. Colonel Towneley, of the Manchester Regiment, volunteered to stay - he was appointed Governor of Carlisle - and maybe many of the Englishmen were relieved not to be going into Scotland. Perhaps it was the Scots, discarded on the doorstep of their own country, who felt most wretched at being left. Maybe Prebble's hope should be accepted. Bonnie

Prince Charlie's humane record is admirable, especially his treatment of prisoners.

Nine of the twenty English officers left at Carlisle, plus the chaplain, and fourteen of the English rank and file were executed. (Seventy-seven Jacobites were executed after the Forty-five. Most of the executions, thirty-three, took place in Cumbria, at Carlisle, Penrith and Brampton. There were twenty-two at both York and London.) If the proselytising John Daniel had not had a horse to sit on, he would have been another to have been hanged for three minutes, stripped, taken down, hit violently by the hangman if there was a twitch of life, cut open, his heart and bowels taken out and thrown on a fire, and his head struck off by a butcher's cleaver. Even such atrocity demonstrated a mercy by the men who did the gruesome work, as Daniel would have been sentenced to be taken down when still alive, his body slashed open so that his bowels could be removed and burned before his face, then his head cut off and his body quartered. Such was the sentence read out to these men, left behind in a cavalier fashion, their value thrown away.

Daniel was at the rainy battle of Falkirk in which his beloved Prince commanded better than Lord George Murray. He helped to count the dead, near seven hundred of the enemy, he said. At Crieff, near Drummond Castle, after acrimonious argument it was decided that the army would divide into two for the fall back to Inverness. The Prince and the clansmen would take the high way, and Lord George lead the horse and low country regiments by the coast roads. In dreadful weather this latter division was pursued by Cumberland's army. As they left Nairn the Hanoverians entered it. Daniel said that the Duke of Perth and Colonel O'Sullivan gained immortal honour by bringing out the men in good order from under the very nose of the enemy, and notwithstanding all the firing at them, not a man was lost.

Captain Daniel after Culloden

Daniel was one of those who, after Culloden, gathered at Ruthven and, against advice to surrender, he took to the hills like the Duke.

Hearing that the Duke was at Doctor Cameron's he called there only to be told that the Duke was unwell, and to realise that his English voice raised suspicion that he was a spy, and that on his own he needed to be careful. He slept out under shelves of rock, was usually starving, and spent a distressing time with destitute women and children driven out of their homes by government soldiers from Fort William.

Then he heard of the two French ships and joined others, including the Duke, on the shore; eventually some four hundred were gathered there. They watched the battle between the French and English ships, on the outcome of which their lives depended.

The Duke of Perth, seeing him in such a piteous condition, called to him and embraced him, and said, "Dear Mr Daniel, I am truly sorry for you, but I assure you that you shall go along with me, and if we are so fortunate as to get to France, depend upon it, that I shall always be your friend". They waited, lying on the shore, the Duke, 'poor man, wrapped up in a blanket,' then waded breast high into the waters to board the boats from La Bellone.

Daniel wrote: "In the ship I was in, there raged a contagious distemper, which carried off sixty-seven in twenty-five days: and about the tenth day of our voyage, I saw the body of my friend and patron the Duke of Perth, thrown overboard; which afflicting sight, joined with my violent sickness, I expected would have put an end to my life. But what I thought would have killed me, perhaps contributed to save my life in that pestiferous ship; as my continual vomiting may have hindered anything noxious from taking any effect upon me. But what is very surprising, for twenty-two days I had not one call of nature, which I affirm upon honour".

I would think that it a safe bet that these words were not known to Thomas Drummond's lawyers in the early 1830s. But they had the 1747 letter to the Duke at Biddick from another man on the ship, the Duke's own brother, seemingly proving that the Duke could not have died in 1746.

Chapter 8
The decisive Court of Session

The final round

On 9th May 1834 the Biddick Claimant Thomas Drummond empowered Ephraim Lockhart, Writer to the Signet, 14 Pitt Street, Edinburgh, to be his Mandatory in the Action before the court of Session.

Thomas Drummond was the pursuer and Lady Willoughby d'Eresby the defender with her husband.

The contest was based on written statements, revised on request, examined by a select small court headed by the Lord Ordinary, initially Lord Jeffrey and later Lord Cockburn.

The Defences, dated 5th June 1834, for Lady Willoughby to the Summons, were presented in print. They stated that the whole descendants of James, 1st Duke of Perth, were extinct, and that James Drummond, who assumed the title of 3rd Duke of Perth, died in 1746 without issue; that the pursuer was not heir male to any descendant of the 1st Duke, nor was he connected with them. He had no right to any of the characters which he assumed and any support he had obtained was against the real evidence and surreptitious.

The defender's father, James Drummond of Lundin, created Lord Perth in 1797, was the heir-male by direct lineal descent of John, Earl of Melfort, younger brother of James, 1st Duke of Perth. He had been served heir-male of the 1st Duke in 1766. One of the characters which the pursuer assumed, that of heir-male to Lord Edward Drummond, had been expressly taken up by the defender's father and he had been served heir-male of Lord Edward as long ago as 1760. Since then more than three times the period of vicennial prescription had elapsed. (Vicennial means relating to a period of twenty years, and prescription limitation of the time within which an action or claim can be raised.) Titles were produced including a crown charter in favour of the defender's father sealed and registered in 1785. The defence concluded by asserting that the possession of the titles and estates for a period much exceeding the years of prescription formed a valid and effectual title to exclude the claims of the pursuer.

It soon became evident that 'prescription' might be of overriding importance. The pursuer, the Biddick Claimant, objected to the defender holding the titles and maintained that his 'interruption' was justified. 'Interruption' was the legal term of the step to end the currency of a period of prescription.

On 12th June Lord Jeffrey gave Thomas Drummond ten days to submit further information - a special Condescendence - in support of his objection. The defenders had to answer this within a further ten days. No mention had been made of the 1747 letter; which in fact had not been part of the Summons drawn up by Lockhart, although that was a succeeding stage to obtain the estates after Thomas Drummond had been declared the lawful heir at Canongate on 3rd March where the evidence of the letter was more appropriate.

The condescendence, on behalf of Thomas Drummond, on 20th June, and the Answers of 8th July, led to a request for a revision of both papers. In the Revised Condescendance, dated 4th September, Thomas Drummond's counsel said that no judicial proceedings were ever adopted to ascertain whether the Duke of Perth was dead or not, which seems a worthwhile point, but what followed seemed naively specious: this was that no indictment or other proceeding was raised against the Duke, nor was any verdict finding him guilty of treason or sentence of outlawry obtained, and it was found that he had never been attainted which was affirmed by the House of Lords. But the Attainder Act of 1746 gave the Duke and his brother until 12th July that year to give themselves up otherwise they would be adjudged attainted of high treason. Lord John was attainted; the Duke wasn't because it was generally accepted that he had died in May, and if Thomas Drummond's contention was correct that his grandfather did not die but lived on in Biddick, then he would have been attainted.

The question of "prescription"

On the crucial issue of prescription it was pleaded that before the pursuer could be excluded from the case, his allegations must be shown to be irrelevant and the defender's deeds unchallengeable.

The pursuer alleged that the defender's deeds were obtained on false representations, and that the defender's father personated a character which he did not hold, and that these allegations were sufficiently relevant to prevent his (Thomas Drummond's) exclusion.

In the revised 'Answers' of the defenders it was denied that the 3rd Duke ever went to South Shields, was married and had issue, or that he survived May 1746, and affirmed that the defender's father, Captain James Drummond, stated truly his descent from Lord Melfort, brother of James, 1st Duke of Perth, and denied that the Crown Charter was applied for and obtained in 1785 upon false representation. The pursuer's pleas against the validity and the titles held by the defender and the relative possession were one and all unfounded, and as the titles had been possessed for a period exceeding the years of prescription they formed valid and effectual right to exclude.

The Court had the revised Answers by mid-November and on 6th December Lord Cockburn announced that the parties should appoint counsels for debate. The debate was over by 22nd January (1835), and on the 27th there came the verdict.

It was against the Biddick Claimant, Thomas Drummond.

The verdict

Lord Cockburn's signed verdict reads:

"Edinburgh 27th January 1835. The Lord Ordinary having considered the Record with the relative writings, and heard the counsel for the parties, Sustains the defences founded on the Defenders title to exclude, Assolzier (Early form of absolve) the Defender from the action and Decerns (to decree or adjudge by judicial sentence), Finds the Pursuer liable in Expenses, Appoints an Account thereof to be given in, and, when lodged, Remits to the Auditor to tax the same and Report."

Lord Cockburn wrote an explanatory note, which he initialled. It is given verbatim:

"The title to exclude is founded on the prescriptive title is completed in the person of the Defender.

"The Pursuer's answer to this is, 1st That there was never any title or warrant on which prescription could flow. 2dly that the alleged prescription had been interrupted.

"The first of these pleas rests on the statement that the 24 Geo: III Cap 27 only empowered the Crown to dispose in favour 'of the heir male of John Drummond (the Duke's attainted younger brother who succeeded to the title on the Duke's assumed death in 1746 and died in 1747) who would have been entitled to succeed by the investitures of the said Estate had it not been forfeited;' - that this character truly belonged to the Pursuers predecessor, and now belonged to himself; and that, notwithstanding this Statutory direction, the Crown was misled to convey in favour of the Defenders father to whom that character did not belong. Assuming all this to be true, the Lord Ordinary is of opinion that the Crown Charter and Seisin (feudal possession of an estate in land) formed a sufficient title of prescription; and thus although the Charter referred expressly to the Act of Parliament, and only conveyed in so far as the Crown had power to do so. Because tho the Crown may have been mistaken, still, acting on the authority of a final decree of the Supreme Court, which declared the Defender's father to be the heir male of John Drummond, it did de facto make a grant in favour of this person by name, on which Seisin and possession followed. The objection that it ought not to have done so, or could not do so effectually, has been often repelled in cases stronger than this one. See Buccleugh 30 Nov 1826. Forbes 29 Nov 1827 and Glassford 17th Fey 1829. The case of Buccleugh in particular, decides this one. The Charter may be defective, and may even have preceded a non domino; - but it is the very object of prescription to refute all such objections.

"The alleged interruption is said to have been affected by an action raised in 1805 against the Defender by a person called Charles Edward Drummond. But it is admitted by the Pursuer in the Record that this action was dismissed on the ground that he had no title to the character in which he had raised it."

This belittling reference to Charles Edward Drummond seems to have been made in ignorance of who he was - the titular Earl of Perth and Duke of Melfort. Such ignorance, in a case of some duration concerning Drummond genealogy, is odd. He was a descendant of John, brother of James, the 1st Duke. But the man was no Scotsman!

A report of the Lord Advocate to Lord Peel in 1824 on attainted Scottish peerages says Charles Edward was believed to be an alien without property in Scotland and of doubtful respectability, that he had officiated at the Roman Catholic chapel in Moorfields and subsisted chiefly on the charity of bankers at Charing Cross. Charles Edward was the man who, as Count Melfort, visited Thomas Drummond's aunt, Elizabeth Peters, hoping for her help in his ceaseless quest for acceptance. Maybe, despite being a prelate at the Vatican, he was undistinguished in appearance as well as repute. He had been born, in France, before his parents married - this weakened his claims - and in the 1805 case he seemed to have believed (or pretended) that he was the son and heir of Edward Drummond, son of James, the 1st Duke. Edward died in 1760, without issue it is recorded.

Expenses incurred by the Defender in the case Drummond v Willoughby amounted to £70.7s.8d. Tax was £22.3s.8d giving a total of £92.lls.4d. The biggest items listed by Lady Willoughby's solicitors were to Rutherford, Keay and Jameson for consultation and debate, 12 guineas on both 6th June 1834 and 19th January 1835 plus clerk's fee £1.2s.6d, each subject to 33 and one third % tax. The opening item of 2nd May 1834 was a letter to Lady Willoughby informing her of the action and requesting certain family papers. This was 3s.4d, the usual charge for letter writing.

Expenses, I would think, in preparing Thomas Drummond's protracted claim must have been much greater.

I garnered the Court of Session details from the Scottish Record Office where I saw original documents during four visits to Edinburgh to that office and the National Library of Scotland. The admirable file on Thomas Drummond's claim to the Earldom in Newcastle's Central Library includes a deadpan (and dejected) summary based on information from one of the Newcastle solicitors, J Rawling Wilson. This says that after a patient hearing Thomas Drummond was non-suited. Lady Willoughby advanced that Drummond was not the person he pretended to be; that she was the nearest heir and next of kin to the deceased Lord Drummond, and that she had been in uninterrupted possession of the estates for upwards of sixty years. (Surely this should be fifty years - 1785 to 1835) It was on this last plea that Drummond failed in his Action.

Rawling Wilson commented that after this a second Memorial was addressed to the King in Council praying him to take the case of the petitioner into consideration. The answer was that the case was not cognisable by the King in Council, and it was recommended that the regular steps should be taken before a committee of privileges. The answer could well have evoked a hollow mirthless laugh and a shrug of horror at the effort, time and expense of that useless roundabout. So the legal case ended.

The question of identity

In the written pleadings, whether or not the Duke died on shipboard in May 1746 was not given major attention. We don't know what came up in debate, although there is no indication in comments afterwards that proof to support statements of early or late death became significant. Much attention went to the granting of the estates to Captain James Drummond in 1785, and Thomas Drummond's protests were dismissed.

The 1747 letter was not mentioned in the written pleadings. Was it, at this final stage, regarded with suspicion by Thomas' counsel? That the claim was decided upon 'prescription' - on the length of time Lady Willoughby's family had held the estates - was a profound disappointment to those who had expected a probing examination into the identity of the man at Biddick.

Obviously Thomas Drummond's lawyers had not realised the immediate entrenched strength of prescription given by the Crown Charter, a strength which endured even if the Crown had been mistaken in granting the Charter. Lord Cockburn said that cases even stronger than that of Thomas Drummond had often been repelled because of prescription.

Prescription means a right created by lapse of time, or a right extinguished by lapse of time. Positive prescription goes back to Roman law. In Scots law it fortifies the title of one who has possessed land for stated periods. In an addendum to the main presentation of Thomas Drummond's case, the one of 1828, questions for counsel, seeking assurance and guidance, were suggested:

Did the evidence justify the case going forward, bearing in mind that the forfeited estates were granted by George III to Captain James Drummond who had been found by a Decree of the Court of Session to be the nearest heir male of John Drummond, (brother of our Duke); and if so what course should be pursued to obtain possession of the estates?

Taking into account all the work done in the compilation of the claim the questions were phrased respectfully, modestly and sensibly. Surely, after advice, the issue of prescription came to the forefront. Its power shown at the Court of Session makes the proportion in the axiom that possession is nine-tenths of the law seem modest. Its power in this Scottish hearing was breathtaking. Lord Cockburn's remarks that even if Biddick Claimant Thomas Drummond was entitled to the succession, and even if the Crown had been misled to convey in favour of Lady de Eresby's father, assuming all this was true, he was still of the opinion that a sufficient title of prescription had been formed.

The two verdicts at the Canongate Court in favour of Thomas being nearest and lawful heir seemed to carry little weight. Also the advisers of Thomas appear to have dismissed too quickly the reports of the Duke's death at sea, although almost certainly they did not know of Daniel's account, and at the time the bulk of research into the Forty-five was still to come. Such research was boosted when that great collection of oral accounts, The Lyon in Mourning, gathered by the Reverend Robert Forbes, was made available, but that was many years ahead. Having said that, in the late 1820s, a man who knew his way around sources and books, the gifted Sir Walter Scott, in Tales of a Grandfather, wrote about the rebellion in detail and with understanding of its course and characters.

But, in the end, in the legal claim of Thomas Drummond, possession was the main key. One could infer that the Court of Session doubted that the man at Biddick was the Duke, but they didn't categorically say that he wasn't.

In 1891 at the Newcastle Leader office in High Bridge, Newcastle, a reprint was made of Thomas Drummond's case at the suggestion, I assume, of his eldest son, James. I saw a copy in the University of Durham's Palace Green library. I had never come across any reference to it. James is entered as twenty in the 1841 census, thirty-three in the 1851 when he was married with two daughters, so this would be a late gesture out of the reflections of old age. A gesture is all it seems to have been, maybe done in the hope that someone influential would became interested. The case was not brought up to date. The reprint is that of the claim first published in 1830 plus the shortened version presented in the petitions to the House of Lords in 1830 and 1831. An addition of a few words says that old Biddick Claimant Thomas was the father of the new claimant, James. There is no explanation of hope or intention.

Chapter 9
The evading title, the questioned letter, the continental valediction

The Lord John Drummond heirs claim - 1750

The claim on the estates at the Court of Session was made as it was the only way forward. The titles could not be used effectually because of attainders - that of 1716 on the Duke's father, and that of 1746 on the Duke's brother, Lord John Drummond. The Duke was assumed to have died before his attainder came into effect, although if he were really the man at Biddick then there would be his attainder too. The attainders on the Drummond family were not reversed until 1853 when George Drummond became de facto Earl of Perth.

The Court of Session's verdict in favour of the incumbents shows that their position was assessed too lightly by believers, and by advisers, in Thomas Drummond's cause. After the death, assumed or otherwise of our 3rd Duke in 1746; of the death, without doubt, of his younger brother, Lord John in 1747, both seemingly without male issue, the succession had gone back a generation to an uncle of half blood, also called John, son of the 1st Duke by his second wife. An active Jacobite, with his half-nephew, the 3rd Duke, John was among the seven who formed the Association or Concert of gentlemen pledging themselves to support Prince Charles when he landed. But in 1745 he was sixty-six, and although the Prince stayed two nights at his house in February 1746 he was not prominent in the rebellion and was not attainted. In Noble British Families he is designated 4th Duke/7th Earl - one short in each instance of his usual designation - by excluding Lord John, our Duke's brother, from the succession on the grounds that being attainted he was counted as dead in law.

During the time our Duke's Uncle John held the titular title, there was in

1750 a remarkable attempt to claim the titles and the forfeited estates by another Thomas Drummond - Thomas Drummond of Logie-Almond. It affirms yet again the inevitability of the Duke of Perth taking up arms in support of the Stuarts and of an understandable but devious plan of his to salvage something from his estate in the event of the rebellion being put down.

In spite of two attainders the estate had been saved by early dispositions in favour of eldest sons. John had no son so he drew up a disposition in favour of Thomas Drummond of Logie-Almond, without telling Thomas.

This was in June 1743 shortly after one of his York Jacobite trips. It was described as a latent deed to be produced in case of need, but it was never actually delivered by Lord John. This Thomas Drummond, it appears, knew nothing at all of the matter, until the rebellion was over. In an explanatory preamble to the disposition Lord John said:

"As I considering that I am frequently very sickly and tender in my constitution and having some thoughts of retiring from the world the better to prepare me for a future state and also considering that John Drummond, my only brother german is now captain in the regiment of Roth in France, is abroad in the army and in foreign service whereby his being married and his capacity of succeeding me in my estate may be very dubious and uncertain, and that I am resting and owing to several persons very considerable sums of money that ought in justice equally to be payed, therefor and for other weighty motives and considerations ..."

If the rebellion was defeated and he escaped then the grantee and his heirs would be bound to pay him two hundred pounds sterling a year. There were also yearly payments to be made to Lord John, and larger ones to his mother, and sister, Lady Mary.

This Thomas Drummond's claim of 1750 was against the Crown, holders of the Perth estates. The verdict was that the estate had gone to Lord John after the 3rd Duke's death, and with Lord John being attainted the estate was forfeitable, and that the disposition to Thomas Drummond of Logie-Almond was not sufficient to exclude this forfeiture and therefore his claim was dismissed. The Crown's defence said that it bore the marks of a fraudulent device, made with the intent to hinder or defraud the king of the forfeiture of the lands.

If the man at Biddick was indeed the 3rd Duke would he not have got a message through to this Thomas Drummond as soon as he was able to arrange it? Or was it not worth the risk? Two hundred pounds a year would have meant comparative affluence at Biddick.

The Duke's Uncle John, despite marrying twice, died childless in 1757. The titular titles then went sideways to another half-uncle, Edward Drummond, son of the 1st Duke by his third wife. Born in 1690 when his parents were incarcerated in Stirling Castle, he was a member of the Jacobite court in France and took part in the 1715 Rising. He was not attainted, and died, childless, in Paris in 1760. The issue male of his father, James, the 1st Duke, now became extinct and the Dukedom succession ceased.

The Melfort heirs claim 1781

Within the lifetime of the man at Biddick the Earldom succession went to yet another, the 10th Earl, by a switch to the heirs of the brother of James, the 1st Duke, that is John Drummond, created Duke of Melfort by the deposed James II. His first marriage was to the heiress of Lundin, in Largo, Fife, and children of that marriage took the name of Lundin, and the Protestant religion of that family.

The succession in 1760 went to his grandson, James Lundin, who immediately returned to the name of Drummond. Two of James Lundin's sons, both unmarried, died within his lifetime: one in the Bermudas after being taken prisoner in the American war.

Lundin-Drummond's third and youngest son, Captain James Drummond, born in 1744, who joined the army in 1771 and was a captain in the 42nd Highlanders in the East Indies, became the titular 11th Earl of Perth in 1781 on the death of his father, and in 1785 received the grant of Drummond Castle and the Perth estates when their annexation by the government was lifted. He had to accept a government exchange of land from the estate for land belonging to the Earl of Breadalbane. The captain was indebted to the sustained intercession of a fellow countryman, Henry Dundas, Secretary of State, later Lord Melville, who strove to keep the estates in Scottish hands.

This was the time of real opportunity for a claim from Biddick. There was no mountain of prescription then. The assumed Duke at Biddick had died in 1782, but his eldest son failed to test the opportunity, either because of ignorance about the annexation coming to an end; apathy; assuming success was impossible; disbelief in his father's case or fright at embarking on the enormous procedure.

Shortly after being granted the estates, Captain Drummond married Clementina, daughter of Lord Elphinstone. In 1797 he was created Lord Perth, Baron Drummond of Stobhall, county Perth, a full British title. Unfortunately for its continuance his only son died at the age of seven in 1799 and the captain died within a year in July 1800 at the age of fifty-six at Drummond Castle. The brief barony became extinct. His widow died in 1822 at Park Lane, Middlesex. This address gives light to an explanation of the meeting in London with the two daughters of our Duke in 1806.

The estates were held by the widow and her daughter Clementina Sarah Drummond, known for a time as Lady Gwydyr but who was Lady Willoughby de Eresby at the time of the Court of Session hearing. The titular Earldom title switched around elsewhere, fluttering briefly on the shoulders of James Louis Drummond, descendant of John Drummond, the 1st Earl and Duke of Melfort, by his second marriage. To the uncertainty posed by interpretations of the attainders there was added the knowledge that James Louis was born four years before his parents wed. However he died in September 1800, and the title moved to his brother, Charles Edward Drummond, already mentioned.

The George Drummond claim 1846

Born in 1752 at Lussan in Languedoc, Charles Edward Drummond became a senior law clerk in the papal service and died in Rome in 1840 at the age of eighty-eight. The title caused Charles Edward some exacerbation, as the precious substance, the estates, had gone to Captain James Drummond and family, and Charles Edward believed the captain to be an impostor. When he called upon Mrs Peters for her help he was probably preparing his 1823 case.

Charles Edward was challenged, unsuccessfully, by his younger brother, Leon Maurice, on the ground that he alone of the brothers was born after his parents' marriage and was the only one legitimate. He was succeeded by his nephew Captain George Drummond, son of the legitimate Leon Maurice, and on 28th June 1853, one hundred and eight years after the Forty-five, the attainders which that and the Fifteen had brought about, were at last reversed. On 19th July that year George Drummond, became de facto Earl of Perth (the fourteenth) and also Earl of Melfort.

But even when the Earl of Perth title was real it was not accompanied by the estates. The change from heirs male to heirs general, seemingly negotiated to keep the estates in Scottish hands, plus the law of prescription strengthened by even more years, saw to that. In 1888 the estates were inherited by the Earl of Ancaster, Lady de Eresby's grandson. George Drummond died in his ninety-fifth year in 1902, outliving his two sons by many years. One, who poisoned himself when twenty-seven, had resigned his commission in the 42nd Highlanders following a charge of cowardice or insubordination during the Crimean war, when he was twenty. The Earldom devolved on the 9th Viscount Strathallan as collateral heir male. In 1996 the Earl of Perth was the seventeenth and had acquired the Perth family's old home, the 16th century castle of Stobhall.

The Biddick Claimant denounced

The 1747 letter from Lord John Drummond was remembered in George Drummond's petition before the Lords Committee of Privileges. During the proceedings the Biddick Claimant Thomas Drummond was denounced as an impostor who had brought forward the pretended original letter from Lord John Drummond to the Duke of Perth to prove that the Duke could not have been drowned in 1746.

"The false pretensions of the Newcastle pitman were completely shown," although the letter and the attendant depositions of its genuineness were said to be the inventions of a designing attorney, as a person in such low condition of life as Thomas Drummond could not have got up such evidence.

The reference, in Noble British Families, fulminates, is biased and is careless. It says that Thomas was the son of a labourer in the coalpits of Newcastle, and that his alleged ducal grandfather settled in Newcastle and worked for a Scotch grocer whose daughter he married; that Thomas had not the means to prosecute his claim (which reveals ignorance of the Canongate Court and the Court of Session hearings), and that Captain James Drummond behaved liberally to him, giving him money at various times.

There was no reference in the local press to the course and verdict of the 1834/35 Court of Session case, despite their expressed anticipation at the beginning. That is, I have not been able to find any in the Durham County Advertiser, the Newcastle Journal and the Newcastle Chronicle. Was the dropping of editorial interest due to disillusion? Had it got around in such circles that the authenticity of the 1747 letter was doubtful? It must have been asked, why was it not at hand when the claim was first being put together in 1826?

If it could not be found, surely it was known and merited mention. Would not the Duke's daughters know of it? If it was a concoction, then late 1826 to 1828 would appear to be the period when it was perpetrated. It was first mentioned in the Claim of 1828. Fitz Strathern, the London law genealogist, drops out of the case after that. He had been very conscious that he was doing research without pay, and understandably was pressing for financial help.

The doubts about the letter

South Biddick was in the parish of Houghton-le-Spring: one can surmise that Fitz Strathern, knowing that because of his hunt for certificates, used it in the phrase "as I find you are living in obscurity at Houghton-le-Spring," - but this is just speculation. The sentence: "I doubt that is a dangerous place yet," sounds idiomatic and the idiom could well be recognised in some English region. The more one looks at that letter the less credible it becomes, although it does not look like the personal invention of a "designing attorney."

In 1828 there seem to have been two factions in the Biddick camp. The second printing of the Claim included a complaint that the first printing, which had been taken from the folio copy produced for private use by Thomas Drummond and his advisers, had included a preparatory address purporting to be written by Thomas. He had not written it, and the printing had not his consent. Also an account of attainted peerages of Scotland was an unwanted interpolation. Neither of these additions seems to be exceptionable in any way, but their insertion and public objection is evidence of people working against each other.

It was stated in support of the letter that Prince Charles often mentioned that the Duke of Perth was alive in England. As far as I know there is no evidence of this. So many reputable historians have sifted through Stuart correspondence and memoirs, and Prince Charles Edward has been subjected to such meticulous research, that his knowledge of the deception would have been commented upon.

Another letter

Others aboard the ship, men going into exile and prone to write, at some time, of their experiences, never mentioned that the Duke hadn't died on the ship, that he hadn't even been on the ship, but was seeking refuge in a God-forsaken part of England. There is further confirmation that the Duke died at sea - was lost in the crossing - in a note in Noble British Families.

"Copie d'une lettre au Ministre de la Marine 7 Juin, 1746.
Monseigneur,
J'ai l'honneur de vous informer de l'arrivee des fregates Le Mars et La Bellone a Painboeuf d'hier - ils ont perdu dans le traversee M. le duc de Perth.
Signe Duteillan (Ordonnateur de la Marine)."

The date of return of the two ships, after their dreadful journey, is usually given as 27th May with up channel Nantes as the port. Painboeuf or Paimboeuf is nearer the mouth of the Loire, nearer to St Nazaire. The dates discrepancy will, surely, be due to the Gregorian calendar, in use in Roman Catholic countries but not accepted by Britain until 1752.

The report is an extract from a letter from the marine commander at Nantes to the Minister in Paris. A copy of it was brought before the Lords Committee for Privileges in 1846 when they began hearing the petition of George Drummond, le Duc de Melfort, to be accepted as Earl of Perth. In it Duteillan also says that Lord Drummond (the Duke's brother) came over in Le Mars and that he, Duteillan, immediately offered him and another gentleman help on the Minister's behalf but the captain of the ship, M. Wailch, said he would see to their every need.

People had suspected that the Prince was on the frigate, but the captain - who would be writing to the minister with many specific details - had assured him that such was not the case. The captain had also told him that the assistance sent over on the frigates had been duly unloaded in Scotland. This was a shipment of arms and ammunition and five barrels of gold - forty thousand louis d'or.

It came far too late, of course. Part of it, known as Cluny's treasure, was concealed in Loch Arkaig for nine years under the care of Cluny Macpherson. The letter was presented to the Lords committee to give proof of the death of the Duke of Perth after he had been wounded at Culloden When it was confirmed that it had been compared with the original held in the Ministry of Marine in Paris, and also stated that the Duke of Perth had been an officer in the French Service, the letter was accepted by the committee.

With no Prince Charles Edward aboard, the return of the privateers caused dismay. King James could not understand why they had returned from Scotland without his son. The Prince had left Loch nan Uamh only six days before the arrival of the ships, and but for the grievous naval battle they would have gone over to Uist to search for him. They were in no condition to do so afterwards - Le Mars had taken seventy-two hits - and there was the possibility of further battle. When the Prince, on South Uist, learned that the ships had been so near and yet failed to cross to look for him, he was upset and angry.

The Latin epitaph on the monument to the Duke of Perth is given in Noble British Families. The monument, in the Convent of English Nuns in Antwerp where his brother Lord John was buried, states that the Duke died at sea on 13 May 1746 at the age of thirty-three:-

Verum assiduis laboribus et patriae malis gravi-
bus oppressus in mari magno die natali revertente
ob. 13, maji 1746, aet 33, et reliquiae ventis adver-
sis terra sacrata interclusae, in undis sepultae

In 1847 during a further hearing of George Drummond's eventually successful petition, a witness told how he and George Drummond found that the old convent in the Rue Houblorinere was being used as a merchant's premises. The burial vaults were a store cellar. Not a fragment of the monument could be found. It seems both brothers were remembered on it, but not for all that long. In 1794 the convent, a community of Carmelite or Teresian nuns, moved to England, to Llanherne, near to St Columb in Cornwall. They brought with them their book of secular burials at the Antwerp convent and that of le Duc de Perth is entered on 28th September 1747. This would be Lord John.

George Drummond's victory 1853

The petition of George Drummond before the Lords Committee for Privileges began in 1846, on 23rd July.

The printed evidence for that first hearing covers 285 pages with the prepared and major part in Latin. A continuation of custom beyond common sense. Comments and questions are in English. The letter from the Minister of Marine at Nantes to the Minister of Marine in Paris in which the death of the 3rd Duke of Perth at sea on board Le Mars is reported was received by the committee.

A summary of the unsuccessful claim of Thomas Drummond of Logie-Almond in 1750 was heard and during this their lordships agreed that the Duke had been allowed until 12th July 1746 to surrender. As he died at sea on 11th May the conditional attainder could not take place and so he was not attainted. He had died without lawful issue and the estate had descended to his brother, John, who was attainted and so it became forfeitable.

That hearing was adjourned sine die. In the next one, the following year, between 20th April and 11th May 1847, counsel for George Drummond stated that since the commencement of proceedings Thomas Drummond of Biddick had presented a petition to the House - I have seen no other reference to this - and that he, George Drummond's counsel, was prepared to prove that in 1835 this Thomas Drummond took proceedings in the Court of Session in Scotland to reduce all the services which established the right of the Lundin branch to represent the Perth family and to the Letters Patent granting the estates to the late Lord Perth, and that the Court pronounced a decree dismissing the action.

There was a further hearing in June and a final one for the time being the following year, on 11th August, when it was agreed that George Drummond had not made out his claim to the titles. The hearings from 1846 to 1848 were chaired by the Earl of Shaftesbury. Other evidence for accepting the death of the Duke of Perth on shipboard in addition to the report from Nantes to the Minister of Marine in Paris and the inscription on the monument in Antwerp, were a judgement in 1752 on a successful claim of Lady Mary Drummond, the Duke's sister, to some estates, the finding on the claim of Thomas Drummond of Logie-Almond, and letters from John styled the 5th Duke of Perth.

In the next hearing, five years later, on 19th July 1853, with Lord

Redesdale in the chair; counsel for George Drummond stated that when the case was last before them the committee had intimated that proof of pedigree was perfectly satisfactory, and that the claim had failed because of the attainder against Lord John Drummond. (All attainders against the Perth family were reversed in 1853 and the hearing followed.)

The Lord Advocate for the Crown stated proof of pedigree appeared to be perfectly satisfactory and so it was agreed that George Drummond, Duke de Melfort and Comte de Lussan in France had made out his claim to the honours and dignities of Lord Drummond, Earl of Perth, Earl of Melfort, Viscount Forth, and the Scottish peerages of Lord Drummond of Rickertoun, Castlemain and Gastoun.

That 1853 decision seems effectively to have settled the possession of the titles.

Chapter 10
If not the Duke, who was he?

The case for the Biddick Duke

Could the Duke of Perth have settled into life at Biddick?

An obvious doubt, it is glanced at in the Claim, concerns the Duke allowing his eldest son to become a pitman, but this is easily dismissed.

Could the 3rd Duke with his background of Jacobite court life from infanty, and rich aristocratic living in Perthshire, accept that rough, limited life, for the first two or three years in a cottage with a pitman and his family?

Prior to Biddick his life of campaigning and fighting had been hard and sometimes brutal, and could have left some coarsening, but he had been a privileged combatant, cushioned when possible, by servants. Also his experiences could have confirmed rather than lessened the class division.

The only way I have thought it credible for him to live on at Biddick was to speculate that Culloden changed him. That, with his dreams shattered, his thinking and feelings took a new direction. As he recovered he could have found that the allure of the Stuart cause had vanished, and that slaughter sickened him. That he was in reaction to what he had been; feeling that he had been a victim of family fanaticism, typified by his obsessed mother. His inner self had changed. His spirited assuredness had gone; leaving him, in effect, not much of a man, and, without the challenge of fighting and working for a long cherished cause, physically frail.

The Hanoverian General Lambton saw that and treated him disdainfully, regarding him from the plateau of his arrogance as not worthy of time and effort to investigate. He was lost and broken, because when certain in his glory, he had been wrong.

What the Biddick Duke wanted was a quiet life, in obscurity, away from all he had known. He would just go along with things. Be married in a Protestant church. Let his children be baptised there. The living was a penance, although there were times of acceptable life vouchsafed to him by a young lovely gentle soothing woman.

I've wondered how he coped with her dialect. Even nowadays, people brought up in the North-east, never mind a Scotsman brought up in France, can find it difficult to make sense of broad local dialect. J R Leifchild in his 1842 report on the employment of children in North-east collieries said the pitmen's language was unintelligible to a stranger. However, a gentle manner of talking could have worked wonders.

Another explanation

When the 1828 claim was being compiled, Mrs Ann Atkinson, the Duke's eldest child, gave evidence that General Lambton said that her father was 'the rebel Drummond' and that he would have him beheaded, and she said, as beheading was only for the nobility, the general must have known of her father's rank. If Lambton knew the man was the Duke of Perth, would he, unless he was wanting to be insulting, have called him "rebel Drummond"? And Nicholas Lambton's words: 'I know you well enough - you are one of the Drummonds, the rebels, but I will give you the house and garden for all that,' imply speaking to one of the clan, not to the titled and distinguished and honourable head. Another indication of this is that he did not change his name.

And would not the Duke's two daughters, Anne and Elizabeth, have tales to tell of occasional outbursts in French, of descriptions of the Jacobite court, of privileged living at Drummond Castle, of moments and incidents and people of the Forty-five?

Drummond could well have been the true name of the man at Biddick.

What could be an initial link in the whole story is that the Duke's equipage was lost at Culloden. Or rather it was lost to him.

Unless smashed by artillery fire, which is unlikely, it would not be lost to everyone. Someone could have taken some of his papers. Maybe it wasn't simply theft, but the saving of them by a servant, who carried them with him in his own escape to England. The Duke's principal servant, present at Culloden, was also called Drummond, but John not James. Might not such a servant, after hearing of the Duke's death at sea, and with these papers in his possession, have been tempted to begin playing the part of the Duke?

Such imaginings in dour surroundings would give him a pride, an importance, an entertainment. And, he could think, he was harming no one. He must confine his tale within his family and close friends. There was still danger beyond the mining community as the irate warning from the Hanoverian General Lambton was to show.

The servant could have sustained a hand wound at Culloden, far from uncommon in that kind of fighting, and, in his old age, visited the estate where he had lived and worked. Perhaps his eldest son, James, was not supine at all, but a hard-working mother's boy, bringing money into the household from an early age, and who regarded his father as an idler, a man who evaded hard and rough money-earning, and who indulged in day dreams and gave them shape with supposed facts to justify, in part, that evasion.

James could have known that his father was a fake. He could have seen his sisters' giggly romantic dreams become hard-headed scheming. As for his impetuous young brother William, well he had got away from the family and felt he was a man of consequence and was not one to let such a prospect fade away unchallenged.

One wonders why the Duke at Biddick, if such he was, did not change his name. He was used to subterfuge, and had been known as Graham and then as Fergus, the latter as recently as 1744. Prince Charles used many pseudonyms. The fact that the man at Biddick did not change his name of Drummond, could indicate that he was a servant and saw no reason to change.

My feeling that he could have been the Duke's servant was boosted when I read in A K Smith's The Noblest Jacobite of All that his principal servant was called John Drummond. Further information from A K Smith killed this convenient stand-in for the real Duke. John Drummond, the Duke's servant for five and a half years, gave testimony in an inquiry into a laird missing since Culloden, and it appears that this was in 1749 in Edinburgh - the year of Drummond's marriage at Biddick. Also he says he went aboard the Mars of Nantz, (not La Bellone as Daniel states), with the 3rd Duke on 3rd May 1746, and that he was never absent from his master from Culloden until his death above half an hour at a time, and in that all the time the Duke was in a weak and sickly condition.

Another deponee in the same inquiry, an Edinburgh man called John Bain, says that he helped the Duke into the French boat. I feel that one has to accept the accumulating evidence that in fact the Duke, when a very sick man, got aboard one of the two French privateers at Loch nan Uamh and that he died on the ship and that he was dropped overboard. John Daniel's account has an authentic ring. It does not look as if it was added by to him, or by someone after his death. If the account was an addition, on request, I think it would have been a little longer, more defined, more detailed. I accept it because this is the death of an aristocrat whom Daniel respected and loved and who gave him friendship, and yet in the telling of that death his own miserable condition of sickness and extreme constipation competes with it for importance.

Scottish spies

Also I have been wondering about a man who it seems was a servant or messenger of the Duke and said even to be a confidant, who was picked up at Southwick, near Sunderland in 1745, at a time, after Prestonpans, when the Jacobites were moving south to England and were stretching out feelers for support.

Southwick, now part of Sunderland, was a separate community in the eighteenth century, on the north bank of the Wear over two miles from the mouth, its old name of Sudick in a transitional state of Southic. In letters of the time, George Grey of Southwick, writing to his brother, a rector in Bedford, tells of his plans to improve his agricultural land and the disruption of living which the Jacobites were causing. There was relief that the North-east had been spared the threatened advance down the east coast.

The main fear was an invasion by the French. Southwick had nearly a thousand militiamen, and nearly a hundred cannon, and its walls were being repaired. Grey says the 'spy' had a letter from the Pretender inviting friends in Yorkshire and Lancashire to join him, and that it was whispered that the names of such gentlemen were known. The night after the spy's apprehension, he had cut his throat but not fatally, and he was likely to recover. I think the letter would have been more likely written by the Duke of Perth, who had been confident of active support in England. In Desperate Factions? Leo Gooch tells of the Duke writing to the Lawsons of Brough inviting them to join the Jacobite army. There was no reply. Maybe the messenger was en route to Brough. I'm wondering if he was held in the Wear area and when freed walked the short distance up river to Biddick.

And how about the man in Wensleydale? Two servants of the Duke were taken prisoner in the trouble at Kendal during the retreat. One may have escaped or been freed, and disappeared out of the way eastward into the Pennines and found himself in the serenity and safeness of Wharfedale and Bishopdale. Almost certainly he would be of the Drummond clan.

Edward Hughes in his North Country Life in the 18th Century writes of the seasonal migration of 'country fellows' from Perth and Falkirk to work in the keels during the shipping season - there were many coal staithes in the Biddick area. Robert Drummond, the Sunderland highwayman, came from Perth. Sentenced to transportation for life he escaped and resumed his night-time activities in the south where one of his robber companions was called James Drummond. Both Drummonds were hanged at Tyburn in February 1730.

Further evidence that Scotsmen at the time migrated to the Biddick area was provided by the death in 1833 at Washington, just north of Biddick, of Andrew Wallace, at the age of 103. Born at Inverness on 14th March 1730, he was with the Jacobite army at Culloden when he was sixteen. A word with him during the second half of the eighteenth century about the man at Biddick could have been revealing.

Some conclusions

I think this man at Biddick, of whom we don't know very much, had probably been with the Jacobite forces at Culloden; that James Drummond was his real name; that late in life he visited the Duke's Perth estates where he had lived, and that he could well have been a servant of the Duke.

I think initially he had some documents belonging to the Duke and that these were lost in the 1771 floods. I think my fancy that he allowed fantasies to develop is feasible. I'd say he wasn't a man used to hard physical work.

A problem is the length of time between his arrival and beginning to earn some money as a ferryboat-man. Why should John Armstrong, the pitman, have given this unknown Scotsman not only shelter but sustenance? Why should Armstrong work down the pit to support him, not just for a week or so, but for a few years? Elizabeth was twelve when he arrived, and apart from mention of an attempt to be a seller of shoes, there is no report of his earning anything until their marriage four or five years later. What, I suggest, is likely is that this man had money and that he paid Armstrong. Why not in addition to some papers, some money from the abandoned equipage? Of course, it could as easily be put forward that because he had money he was the Duke.

The marriage at St Michael's Church, Houghton-le-Spring, was on 6th November 1749. Anne, the first child, was christened at the same church on 10th June 1750, so when they married Elizabeth was pregnant.

Their second child and first boy, James, baptised at Houghton on 9th August 1752, has been dismissed as a wimpish mother's boy, turning away into his hard work at the pit when frightened at the bewildering effort required to begin trying to regain his family's rights. He was thirty when his father died in 1782, and two years later when the annexation was lifted had the best opportunity of gaining the estates, but he was inept. That could be near the truth. On the other hand he could have known doing something was useless, that his father was a ne'er-do-well dreamer riding on the backs of people who had to be practical.

But how about the 1747 letter? I wondered if the supposed Duke himself could have written it as part of the evidence to support his fantasy, but if that were so its presence, or the fact that it had been written, would have been known and mentioned earlier. That applies too if it had been the work of both or one of his daughters, especially of Mrs Elizabeth Peters, eager to take action after the death of her brother in February 1823, and looking to his eldest son, Thomas, to be the prow of the venture. Thomas, at first, was uninterested. Without Mrs Peters, fourteen years younger than Anne, there would not have been the initial enthusiasm and belief to begin seriously assembling the claim. Maybe she said to Fitz Strathern that she was sure that there had been a letter from her father's brother in the lost papers.

The fall of the Biddick Claimant

James Drummond, and Margaret Pearson from Lambton nearby, parents to be of Thomas, were married at Penshaw chapel of ease, All Saints' Church, on

2nd April 1776. Thomas was born sixteen years later on 3rd April 1792, and baptised at Penshaw church on 17th June. He never knew his ducal grandfather, and would be fourteen when his two aunts made their first approach to Baroness Perth and daughter. He married Jane Burn of Newbottle on 14th May 1815.

Thomas, the Biddick Claimant, enjoyed his tipple but the price was high if the story is true of Lord Durham withdrawing his support when Thomas was drunk on the eve of appearing before the bar of the House of Lords.

The Sunderland - Durham railway line opened in 1836 with a station at New Penshaw. The Sunderland Borough police were established the following year. Both would assist in the incident reported in the Sunderland Beacon of 22nd August 1839 that:

"Thomas Drummond, alias the Earl of Perth, was charged by Police No 5 with being drunk and disorderly on Saturday night, and, when taken to the Station House, attempted to strike the Officer... The Earl said he had no recollection of it. The Mayor replied that the Bench would bring it to his recollection... He was fined 2s/6d and costs."

The Beacon commented, "Earls and their ladies even today are occasionally fined in the courts." So the verdict of the Court of Session in Edinburgh in 1835 had not wiped out a cherished belief of an Earl in pitman's clothing.

Shortly after that, in the 1841 census, Thomas is entered as a bookseller, in New Painshaw which was being built on the bank up from the river, below old Painshaw. A bookseller in New Painshaw or Penshaw before the middle of the nineteenth century! It is worthy of an exclamation mark. Was that to be the main change the case made on Thomas, one towards reflection and knowledge, and away from dirty and hard and despised work? I can recall when even labourers in an engineering shop looked down on "pit yackers." His age is given as forty-five, instead of forty-eight or forty-nine. Although ten children were named, according to the gravestone dates of death, three more should have been there, two girls and a boy. In addition a baby girl had died.

In the 1851 census with our bookseller now fifty-eight and Jane fifty-five, Margaret the eldest at thirty-four was a milliner, James, the eldest son, aged thirty-three had his own family entry with a wife and two children; and

Thomas, the second son, a carpenter, aged twenty-six, married with three children, also had his own home. Eight children were still at home: John was a sailor; William and Malcolm engine firemen; Maurice and Edward masons, and the two youngest, Annabella, fourteen and Mary, eleven, were scholars.

In 1861, Thomas of Front Row, New Penshaw, sixty-nine, was back to coal mining. To return to that in his sixties would have been hard, but, no doubt, it was better paid. Five children were at home and a grandson. Margaret, aged forty-four and Annabella, were entered as dressmakers. In 1871, the last census for Thomas, his description was: "Out brother of Sherburn Hospital." Jane who died on 2 April 1871, about census time, aged seventy-seven, was described as "Out Brother's wife." William and Malcolm, enginemen, were forty-two and unmarried. Margaret and Annabella had died. Thomas's entry in the burial register at Penshaw church was November 22nd 1873, 81 years, then in small hand, 'alleged Earl of Perth.'

The Duke of Biddick's descendants

There were many descendants, of course, of various names. Under Wearside Echoes on 29th October 1949 in the Sunderland Echo, a reporter tells of meeting Margaret Jane Armstrong, an eighty-six year old widow of Shiney Row, (adjacent to Penshaw), who, he said, might have been a titled lady had her grandfather succeeded in his claim. Her brother, William, aged eighty-two, was living in Houghton-le-Spring. Their father Thomas had worked on the Lambton mineral lines and died in 1916. His work-mates generally referred to him as 'The Earl.' In the 1871 census their father was an agricultural labourer, aged forty-seven which would make him ninety-two on his death. In that census Margaret, aged eight, and William, aged four, were the youngest of four surviving children.

It was a family of disparity in length of life. It is the six young dead of this family who are remembered on the smaller gravestone next to the main Drummond one in Penshaw graveyard. Father Thomas was the second son of Thomas the claimant. James, the first son, married later than his brother and in the 1851 census his two children were both girls, so it could be that the direct male issue descent came to the family of the second son.

Also in the Sunderland Echo in 1949 a correspondent recalled that about

1915 the Reverend Maurice Drummond, who said that he was a descendant of the 6th Earl of Perth, died at Lanchester in County Durham aged eighty-two. In the 1841 census Thomas's sixth son was called Maurice and was eight, so surely it would be he. In the 1851 census, aged eighteen, he was a mason but he was away from New Penshaw before the next census. He became a Primitive Methodist clergyman, which would not have amused the real Duke of Perth. A son a clergyman, himself a bookseller, are indications of change in the life of Thomas, the "common pitman" claimant.

In the 1891 reprint of Thomas's case, James, his eldest son, then living at Biddick Row, Washington, lists five Drummonds of his generation still alive - four younger brothers and a sister They were Thomas of Shiney Row; William of South Hylton, near Sunderland; Malcolm Nicholas of Newbottle; Maurice Andrew of Tadcaster and Mary Henrietta Waite of Shiney Row. Maurice will be the Primitive Methodist clergyman who died at Lanchester.

The boathouse at Biddick was on the north side of the river, the side on which the donor, Nicholas Lambton of North Biddick Hall, later known as Cook's Hall, lived. Albert Hind, the local historian, said the boathouse became known as Girdle Cake Cottage. Its location as a boathouse seems to make sense: just over two hundred yards down river of the site selected generations later for Fatfield bridge, the local road bridge; in an old area of coal staithes and pits on both sides, and where the river begins to bend and is narrower. William Casson's 1801 map of the collieries shows tracks to that position from each side. I can remember when there were summer boat trips up river from Sunderland to the cottage for tea, and surely girdles - as scones were known - were served.

It was a sylvan setting. The signs of old industry had gone. The picturesque cottage was demolished in 1932 and a brutally un-picturesque electricity pumping station plumped in its place. Those were great flush days for electricity. Frederick Hill says the boathouse was next to Girdle Cake Cottage. Nicholas Lambton had another cottage built on or close to the site when the original building was destroyed in the 1771 flood.

I wish I'd had a chat with Albert Hind about the location when I lived at North Biddick. I'd assumed that the Duke's boathouse was a good quarter mile further up river near to a resort of old Biddickers, the Ferryboat Inn, which disappeared in the New Town's ruthless sweep, or a little further up still at Chartershaugh where tracks led to a ford. Certainly in the 1820s, late in the lifetime of the Duke's eldest son, James, the landlord of the Ferryboat was also the ferryman. There could well have been a switch of ferry crossings, of course, with the shifting importance of pits and staithes, or even a duplication. There were times when people crossed the river by stepping their way across and over the side-by-side keelboats.

But confirmation of Albert Hind's deduction came from John Frost, the son of the last ferryman in the area on the crossing down river between Coxgreen and Barmston. He told me that there had been a crossing at Girdle Cake, that there was no doubt about it, and that he had never heard mention of one a little upstream. John Frost's father gave up ferrying. He'd had enough, and since 1958 there's been a metal footbridge over the river at Coxgreen. He was always on call, and late on he upped his charge fifty per cent, from a penny a crossing to three ha'pence - all old money. So our Duke wouldn't get much - a ha'penny at the most, I expect. No wonder his wife ran a little shop.

Ferrying, manoeuvring small rowing boats adroitly in the changing conditions, understandably was often a father to son job, and helping his Dad from an early age could well have led to second son William deciding to go to sea.

Fordyce says that population of South Biddick in 1801 was 490; in 1831 it was 199 and in 1851 it was a community of only 38 people occupying eight houses. Houses had been built at adjacent New Penshaw on the hillside ascending to the new railway station. Nowadays there is a long row of riverside dwellings but the geographical place name South Biddick has faded. So has that of North Biddick extinguished by the growing appetite of Fatfield.

The Biddick Duke's supporters

Those who are going to continue to believe that the man at Biddick was the Duke - their belief is often unshakeable and their number is apt to increase - can point to the inability of people including those around at the time to agree on which ship the Duke was supposed to be on when he died.

Most historians don't name the ship, and are content to say, often in a note, that he died on shipboard when escaping to France.

His principal servant for five and a half years, John Drummond, says he was with him when he died on Le Mars; Evan Charteris in his introduction to

David, Lord Elcho's A Short Account of the Affairs of Scotland 1744 to 1746, says Elcho was on Le Mars with the Duke and the Duke's brother, and the 'gallant Perth died during the voyage and was buried at sea.'

The Lords committee hearing the petition of George Drummond a hundred years after Culloden accepted the information from the marine official at Nantes that the Duke had died on Le Mars. John S Gibson, author of Ships of the '45, says Le Mars, and Lieutenant Frogier who was on that vessel wrote in his memoir that the Duke died on the night of 8 May (yet another date) and his body was buried at sea the following morning before the eyes of his distressed friends and saluted by the guns of Le Mars.

The Dictionary of National Biography and the editors of the Stuart Papers at Windsor say La Bellone, and Daniel, on La Bellone, wrote that he saw the body of the Duke thrown overboard.

I know people can soon became unsure of the name of ships they travel on, but the lack of unanimity - I have never seen it mentioned - is odd. In volume XIII of Scottish Antiquary although the claims of Thomas Drummond were denigrated, a variance of date of death at sea was admitted.

There's also the reaction of the solicitors when first approached by Mrs Peters. There was a mountain of work facing them if they went ahead, there were expenses which they would have to meet and there was no payment for them if they failed, and yet they decided to go ahead - they must have thought the claim was that good. Later they were helped by public subscriptions, and by the local press which seemed to have been convinced that the claim was justified. The talk of Mrs Peters must have been persuasive.

They began the case even with the man who mattered most, Thomas himself, reluctant to be concerned. One feels they didn't enquire enough at first, and later, filled with their own belief, belittled contrary evidence and turned away from investigation which might shake their belief. Toward the end, when prescription reared up, an unassailable mountain, they still went on.

And a further point for believers is Mrs Peters herself. For all we know she may have listened to her father's tales when a little girl, tales which became part of her daily thoughts. She could well have had no doubt at all but that he was a Duke. Unless the Lambtons helped her initially, and there is no reference of this, I imagine she would have to arrange with a friendly carter to give her a lift to Newcastle, unless she walked there, and then set about convincing educated and professional men that her cause was just and strong. And would not there be a request for supporting documents, no matter how inspired she was? Surely the solicitors would not have gone ahead without any. Mrs Peters' feat of persuasion is impressive.

I cannot believe that so many Jacobites participated in a conspiracy sustained in reports even to King James that the Duke was aboard and that he died and was buried at sea, when they knew that he wasn't aboard at all. If there was such a conspiracy, someone, I feel, would have told of it later when it seemed to matter less. The amazingly persuasive Mrs Peters could have been an early victim of a deceit.

A friend whose family married into the Drummond family kindly looked at this script and said that my writing (unwittingly) had convinced him that the man at Biddick was the Duke, that such a man would not fool his daughters. "Why should anyone," he added, "impersonate a man wanted for execution?"

All in all ...

I would have liked to have come to the belief that the man at Biddick was the Duke, but considered that the evidence of death at sea in 1746, despite the differences of date and ship, was too weighty, and also, that unless he had undergone a profound change at and immediately after Culloden, his life and behaviour at Biddick were not credible.

But I think that there was a connection; that the man had been a servant of the Duke, or at least was of the clan Drummond, that probably he had in his possession some Drummond papers, and that possibly Culloden and its aftermath had been a trauma to him which evolved into compensating day-dreams and expression.

TIMELINE

DATE	SCOTTISH FAMILY	BIDDICK FAMILY
1693	James II makes 4th Earl of Perth the 1st Duke of Perth. But James is in exile so it has no validity.	
1713	James Drummond, who will become 3rd Duke of Perth, is born. Brought up in France.	Biddick Duke born ... according to his death certificate 69 years later.
1715	James II's son leads a rebellion to restore his father to the throne. The 2nd Duke fights alongside him. They are defeated and family goes to exile in France.	
1716	The 1st Duke dies in France.	
1720	The 2nd Duke dies. James Drummond becomes 3rd Duke of Perth but stays in exile in France.	
1732	3rd Duke returns to Scotland and Drummond Castle	
1745	Bonnie Prince Charlie lands in Scotland to lead a second Stuart rebellion against English rule. 3rd Duke supports Stuart claim as his father and grandfather had.	
1746	Battle of Culloden. 3rd Duke, James Drummond, flees and dies of wounds on ship to France ...	... or 3rd Duke, James Drummond, flees battle, hides in the woods of his castle then escapes to Biddick and lives in obscurity

DATE	SCOTTISH FAMILY	BIDDICK FAMILY
1747	Lord John Drummond, brother of 3rd Duke, dies (Sept). He is the last of the 1st Duke's line ... unless the 3rd Duke survived Culloden, of course.	Lord John Drummond, brother of 3rd Duke, writes a letter to the Biddick Duke (May). This letter will become important proof that 3rd Duke survived Culloden.
1749		Biddick Duke marries Elizabeth Armstrong, (Nov.) a miner's beautiful daughter, at Biddick and settles there with her as a ferryboat-man.
1750		Biddick Duke's first child born (June). Daughter Anne.
1752		Biddick Duke's first son born. Also called James. He will never claim to be the heir to the Perth titles, but his son will.
1764		Biddick Duke's daughter Elizabeth born. She will be the driving force behind her nephew's claim to the title in 62 years time.
1771		Floods on the Wear wash away family papers and much proof of Biddick Duke's claim
1776		Biddick Duke's son, James, marries Margaret at around the time the Biddick Duke visits his old estates in Perth.
1782		Biddick Duke dies

DATE	SCOTTISH FAMILY	BIDDICK FAMILY
1784	Estates granted to heirs of 1st Duke in the person of Captain James Drummond - but he doesn't get the titles. He is charged £52,000 for the estates but it seems he never ever paid it.	Biddick Duke's son, James, makes no claim on Scottish estates. Younger son (William) decides to make a claim. He takes vital papers to prove the claim. William (and the papers) are lost in a sea tragedy.
1792	Captain James Drummond claims title Baron of Perth to go with the lands. He is made Baron in 1797.	Biddick Duke's grandson, Thomas is born almost ten years after Biddick Duke died. Grandson Thomas will go on to make a claim as the heir.
1800	Captain James dies and his daughter, Clementina Sarah, inherits the Perth estates with her husband, Lord Gwydyr, but not the titles. That goes to a priest, Charles Edward Drummond.	
1806		Biddick Duke's daughters, Elizabeth and Anne, go to London to meet the Scottish Perth family and present their case. Clementina Sarah rejects them.
1815		Biddick Duke's Grandson, Thomas, marries Jane.
1823		James, son of Biddick Duke and father of Thomas, dies
1826		Thomas Drummond begins legal attempt to get himself declared the heir to the Perth lands.

DATE	SCOTTISH FAMILY	BIDDICK FAMILY
1828		The Biddick Claimant produces that 1747 letter to "prove" the 3rd Duke survived Culloden. Why didn't he produce it two years ago? And how did it survive the 1771 disaster?
1830		The Biddick Claimant's petition goes to the king and the House of Lords. No record of the decision.
1831		A second attempt. This time a jury declares Biddick claimant, Thomas, is "nearest and lawful heir" to the title. But he doesn't get the land.
1834	Clementina Sarah accused of being in possession of the Perth estates under false pretences. She hangs on because - right or wrong - her family have been there for over 50 years.	The Biddick Claimant now makes a bid for the Perth estates. He fails to get the Perth wealth but no one tries to argue that he isn't the rightful Duke.
1839		Biddick Claimant reported in Sunderland Beacon newspaper for being drunk and striking a policeman. He is described as "alias the Earl of Perth" ... so he still believes it!
1873		Thomas, the Biddick Claimant dies

BIBLIOGRAPHY

Scottish Record Office, Edinburgh: Court of Session, MS Drummond v Willoughby 1834-35. Minute Books, 1833-35

National Library of Scotland: Parliamentary Papers, House of Lords, George Drummond's Claim to the Earldom 1846 and 1847

Edinburgh City Archives: Canongate Register of Service of Heirs, 1829-31, 1834-36.
House of Lords Record Office: Journal of the House of Lords.

North East libraries: Durham City, Newcastle Central, Sunderland, Tyne and Wear Archives, University of Durham (Palace Green), Washington.

The collection of material at Newcastle was my starting base. It includes the printed claim, also held by other local libraries.

Newspapers: Durham Advertiser, Newcastle Chronicle, Newcastle Courant, Newcastle Journal, Newcastle Weekly Chronicle (all contemporary). Sunderland Echo.

Histories of Durham: Hutchinson 1787; Mackenzie and Ross 1834; Fordyce 1855, Surtees, reprinted 1972

Doubleday, White and de Walden The Complete Peerage 1932 and 1945
Drummond, Henry Histories of Noble British Families

	Scottish Antiquary, Vol. XIII,
Boyle, J R (article)	*Monthly Chronicle of North-country Lore and Legend, 1889*
Cooper, Leonard	*Radical Jack, (The Earl of Durham), 1959*
Hill, Frederick	*The Pitman Earl, of Biddick*
Hind, Albert E	*History and Folklore of Old Washington, 1976*
Hughes, Edward	*North Country Life in the Eighteenth Century, 1952*

Purdon, Gavin   *'Cotia Pit, late 1970s*

Mitchell, W Cranmer   *History of Sunderland, 1919*

Speight, H   *Romantic Richmondshire*

Sutcliffe, Halliwell   *The Striding Dales*

Sykes, John   *Historical Register of Remarkable Events, reprinted 1973*

Blaikie, Walter Biggar (ed.)   *Origins of the '45, 1916*

Duke, Winifred   *The Rash Adventurer, 1952*

Elcho, David, Lord   *A Short Account of the Affairs of Scotland 1744-46,*
                                  ed. Evan Charteris 1907, facsimile 1977

Erickson, Carolly   *Bonnie Prince Charlie, 1993*

Forbes, Rev Robert   *The Lyon in Mourning, 1895-96*

Gibson, John S   *Ships of the '45, 1967*

Gooch, Leo   *The Desperate Factions? The Jacobites of North East*
                                  England, 1688-1745, 1995

Johnstone, Chevalier de   *Memoirs of the Rebellion in 1745 and 1746, 1820*

Mackenzie, Compton   *Prince Charlie, 1932*

Menary, George   *Life and Letters of Duncan Forbes of Culloden, 1936*

Murray, John, of Broughton   *Memorials of, 1898*

Petrie, Sir Charles   *The Jacobite Movement: The Last Phase, 1950*

Prebble, John   *Culloden, 1961*

Scott, Sir Walter   *Tales of a Grandfather, 1828-30*

Smith, A K   *The Noblest Jacobite of All, 1995*

Smith, Annette M   *Jacobite Estates of the Forty-five, 1982*

Tayler, Alistair & Henrietta   *The Stuart Papers at Windsor, 1939*

Tayler, Henrietta   *Jacobite Epilogue, 1941*

Terry, Charles Sanford, ed.   *The Forty-five, 1922*

Tomasson, Katherine and
Francis Buist   *Battles of the '45, 1967*

Wilkinson, Clennell   *Bonnie Prince Charlie, 1932*